YOUR PERSONAL
HOROSCOPE
2018

AQUARIUS

Your Personal Horoscope 2018

Aquarius

21st January–19th February

igloobooks

igloobooks

Published in 2017
by Igloo Books Ltd
Cottage Farm
Sywell
NN6 0BJ
www.igloobooks.com

Produced for Igloo Books by Foulsham Publishing Ltd, The Old Barrel Store,
Drayman's Lane, Marlow, Bucks SL7 2FF, England

FIR003 0717
2 4 6 8 10 9 7 5 3 1
ISBN: 978-1-78670-876-2

This is an abridged version of material originally published
in Old Moore's Horoscope and Astral Diary.

Cover design by Charles Wood-Penn
Edited by Jasmin Peppiatt

Printed and manufactured in China

CONTENTS

INTRODUCTION

Your Personal Horoscopes have been specifically created to allow you to get the most from astrological patterns and the way they have a bearing on not only your zodiac sign, but nuances within it. Using the diary section of the book you can read about the influences and possibilities of each and every day of the year. It will be possible for you to see when you are likely to be cheerful and happy or those times when your nature is in retreat and you will be more circumspect. The diary will help to give you a feel for the specific 'cycles' of astrology and the way they can subtly change your day-to-day life. For example, when you see the sign ☿, this means that the planet Mercury is retrograde at that time. Retrograde means it appears to be running backwards through the zodiac. Such a happening has a significant effect on communication skills, but this is only one small aspect of how the Personal Horoscope can help you.

With Your Personal Horoscope the story doesn't end with the diary pages. It includes simple ways for you to work out the zodiac sign the Moon occupied at the time of your birth, and what this means for your personality. In addition, if you know the time of day you were born, it is possible to discover your Ascendant, yet another important guide to your personal make-up and potential.

Many readers are interested in relationships and in knowing how well they get on with people of other astrological signs. You might also be interested in the way you appear to very different sorts of individuals. If you are such a person, the section on Venus will be of particular interest. Despite the rapidly changing position of this planet, you can work out your Venus sign, and learn what bearing it will have on your life.

Using Your Personal Horoscope you can travel on one of the most fascinating and rewarding journeys that anyone can take – the journey to a better realisation of self.

THE ESSENCE
OF AQUARIUS

Exploring the Personality of Aquarius the Water Carrier

(21ST JANUARY – 19TH FEBRUARY)

What's in a sign?

Oh, what a wonderful person you can be! Despite a number of contradictions and one of the most complicated natures to be found anywhere in the zodiac, you certainly know how to make friends and influence people. Your ruling planet is Uranus, one of the more recently discovered members of the solar system's family. It rules modern communications, such as radio and television, and also has a response to the recent discoveries of science. It is within the world of 'the modern' that you reside and you have little or no difficulty keeping up with the ever-increasing pace of life.

People naturally like you and it's not surprising. You are open, liberal, and rarely judgmental, and you are often surrounded by deeply original and even eccentric types. Life to you is a storybook full of fascinating tales. Aquarians amass information 'on the hoof' and very little passes you by. Understanding what makes others tick is meat and drink to you and proves to be a source of endless joy. Unlike the other Air signs of Gemini and Libra, you are able to spend long hours on your own if necessary and always keep your mind active.

Aquarians have great creative potential; they are refined, often extremely well educated and they remain totally classless. This makes it easy for you to get on with just about any sort of person and also explains your general success in the material world. You are fascinating, original, thought-provoking and even quite deep on occasions. Matters that take months for others to synthesise, you can absorb in minutes. It is clear to everyone that you are one of life's natural leaders, but when you head any organisation you do so by co-operation and example because you are not in the least authoritarian.

In love you can be ardent and sincere – for a while at least. You need to be loved and it's true that deeply personal relationships can be a problem to you if they are not supplying what is most important to you. Few people know the real you, because your nature exists on so many different levels. For this reason alone you defy analysis and tend to remain outside the scope of orthodoxy. And because people can't weigh you up adequately, you appear to be more fascinating than ever.

Aquarius resources

Your chief resource has to be originality. Like a precious Fabergé Egg you are a single creation, unique and quite unlike anything else to be found anywhere in the world. Of course, used wrongly, this can make you seem odd or even downright peculiar. But Aquarians usually have a knack for creating the best possible impression. The chances are that you dress in your own way and speak the words that occur to you, and that you have a side to your nature that shuns convention. Despite this you know how to adapt when necessary. As a result your dinner parties would sport guests of a wide variety of types and stations. All of these people think they know the 'real you' and remain committed to helping you as much as they can.

The natural adaptability that goes along with being an Aquarian makes it possible for you to turn your hand to many different projects. And because you are from an Air sign, you can undertake a variety of tasks at the same time. This makes for a busy life, but being on the go is vital for you and you only tire when you are forced into jobs that you find demeaning, pointless or downright dull.

All of the above combines to make a nature that has 'resourcefulness' as its middle name. Arriving at a given set of circumstances – say a specific task that has to be undertaken – you first analyse what is required. Having done so you get cracking and invariably manage to impress all manner of people with your dexterity, attention to detail and downright intelligence. You can turn work into a social event, or derive financial gain from your social life. Activity is the keyword and you don't really differentiate between the various components of life as many people would.

Success depends on a number of different factors. You need to be doing things you enjoy as much you can and you simply cannot be held back or bound to follow rules that appear to make no sense to you. You respond well to kindness, and generally receive it because you are so considerate yourself. But perhaps your greatest skill of all is your ability to make a silk purse out of a sow's ear. You are never stuck for an idea and rarely let financial restrictions get in your way.

Beneath the surface

'What you see is what you get' could never really be considered a sensible or accurate statement when applied to the sign of Aquarius. It's difficult enough for you to know the way your complicated mind works, and almost impossible for others to sort out the tangle of possibilities. Your mind can be as untidy as a tatty workbox on occasions and yet at other times you can see through situations with a clarity that would dazzle almost any observer. It really depends on a whole host of circumstances, some of which are inevitably beyond your own control. You are at your best when you are allowed to take charge from the very start of any project, because then your originality of thought comes into play. Your sort of logic is unique to you, so don't expect anyone else to go down the same mental routes that you find easy to follow.

Aquarians are naturally kind and don't tend to discriminate. This is not a considered matter, it's simply the way you are. As a result it is very hard for you to understand prejudice, or individuals who show any form of intolerance. The fairness that you exemplify isn't something that you have to work at – it comes as naturally to you as breathing does.

You can be very peculiar and even a little cranky on occasions. These aspects of your nature are unlikely to have any bearing on your overall popularity, but they do betray a rather unusual mindset that isn't like that of any other zodiac sign. When you feel stressed you tend to withdraw into yourself, which is not really good for you. A much better strategy would be to verbalise what you are thinking, even though this is not always particularly easy to do.

There are many people in the world who think they know you well, but each and every one of them knows only one Aquarian. There are always more, each a unique individual and probably as much of a mystery to you as they would be to all your relatives and friends, that is if any of them suspected just how deep and mysterious you can be. Despite these facts, your mind is clear and concise, enabling you to get to the truth of any given situation almost immediately. You should never doubt your intuitive foresight and, in the main, must always back your hunches. It is rare indeed for you to be totally wrong about the outcome of any potential situation and your genuine originality of thought is the greatest gift providence has bestowed on you.

Making the best of yourself

Interacting with the world is most important to you. Although you can sometimes be a good deal quieter than the other Air signs of Gemini and Libra, you are still a born communicator, with a great need to live your life to the full. If you feel hemmed in or constrained by circumstances, you are not going to show your best face to family, friends or colleagues. That's why you must move heaven and earth to make certain that you are not tied down in any way. Maintaining a sense of freedom is really just a mental state to Aquarius but it is absolutely vital to your well-being.

As far as work is concerned you need to be doing something that allows you the room you need to move. Any occupation that means thinking on your feet would probably suit you fine. All the same you feel more comfortable in administrative surroundings, rather than getting your hands dirty. Any profession that brings change and variety on a daily basis would be best. You are a good team operator, and yet can easily lead from the front. Don't be frightened to show colleagues that you have an original way of looking at life and that you are an inveterate problem solver.

In terms of friendship you tend to be quite catholic in your choice of pals. Making the best of yourself means keeping things that way. You are not naturally jealous yourself but you do tend to attract friends who are. Make it plain that you can't tie yourself down to any one association, no matter how old or close it may be. At least if you do this nobody can suggest that they weren't warned when you wander off to talk to someone else. Personal relationships are a different matter, though it's hardly likely that you would live in the pocket of your partner. In any situation you need space to breathe, and this includes romantic attachments. People who know you well will not try to hem you in.

Don't be frightened to show your unconventional, even wild side to the world at large. You are a bold character, with a great deal to say and a natural warmth that could melt an iceberg. This is the way providence made you and it is only right to use your gifts to the full.

The impressions you give

You are not a naturally secretive person and don't hold back very much when it comes to speaking your mind. It might be suggested therefore that the external and internal Aquarian is more or less the same person. Although generally true, it has to be remembered that you have a multifaceted nature and one that adapts quickly to changing circumstances. It is this very adaptability that sets you apart in the eyes of the world.

You often make decisions based on intuitive foresight and although many Aquarians are of above average intelligence, you won't always make use of a deep knowledge of any given situation. In essence you often do what seems right, though you tend to act whilst others are still standing around and thinking. This makes you good to have around in a crisis and convinces many of those looking on that you are incredibly capable, relaxed and confident. Of course this isn't always the case, but even a nervous interior tends to breed outward action in the case of your zodiac sign, so the world can be forgiven for jumping to the wrong conclusion.

People like you – there's no doubt about that. However, you must realise that you have a very upfront attitude, which on occasions is going to get you into trouble. Your occasional weirdness, rather than being a turn-off, is likely to stimulate the interest that the world has in you. Those with whom you come into contract invariably find your personality to be attractive, generous, high-spirited and refreshing. For all these reasons it is very unlikely that you would actually make many enemies, even if some folk are clearly jealous of the easy way you have with the world.

One of the great things about Aquarians is that they love to join in. As a result you may find yourself doing all sorts of things that others would find either difficult or frightening. You can be zany, wild and even mad on occasions, but these tendencies will only get you liked all the more. The world will only tire of you if you allow yourself to get down in the dumps or grumpy – a very rare state for Aquarius.

The way forward

In terms of living your life to the full it is probable that you don't need any real advice from an astrologer. Your confidence allows you to go places that would make some people shiver, whilst your intuitive foresight gives you the armoury you need to deal with a world that can sometimes seem threatening. Yet for all this you are not immune to mental turmoil on occasions, and probably spend rather too much time in the fast lane. It's good to rest, a fact that you need to remember the next time you find yourself surrounded by twenty-seven jobs, all of which you are trying to undertake at the same time.

The more the world turns in the direction of information technology, the happier you are likely to become. If others have difficulty in this age of computers, it's likely that you relish the challenges and the opportunities that these artificial intelligences offer. You are happy with New Age concepts and tend to look at the world with compassion and understanding. Despite the fact that you are always on the go, it's rare for you to be moving forward so fast that you forget either the planet that brought you to birth, or the many underprivileged people who inhabit parts of it. You have a highly developed conscience and tend to work for the good of humanity whenever you can.

You might not be constructed of the highest moral fibre known to humanity, a fact that sometimes shows when it comes to romantic attachments. Many Aquarians play the field at some time in their lives and it's certain that you need a personal relationship that keeps you mentally stimulated. Although your exterior can sometimes seem superficial, you have a deep and sensitive soul – so perhaps you should marry a poet, or at least someone who can cope with the twists and turns of the Aquarian mind. Aquarians who tie themselves down too early, or to the wrong sort of individual, invariable end up regretting the fact.

You can be deeply creative and need to live in clean and cheerful surroundings. Though not exactly a minimalist you don't like clutter and constantly need to spring-clean your home – and your mind. Living with others isn't difficult for you, in fact it's essential. Since you are so adaptable you fit in easily to almost any environment, though you will always ultimately stamp your own character onto it. You love to be loved and offer a great deal in return, even if you are occasionally absent when people need you the most. In essence you are in love with life and so perhaps you should not be too surprised to discover that it is very fond of you too.

AQUARIUS ON THE CUSP

Astrological profiles are altered for those people born at either the beginning or the end of a zodiac sign, or, more properly, on the cusps of a sign. In the case of Aquarius this would be on the 21st of January and for two or three days after, and similarly at the end of the sign, probably from the 17th to the 19th of February.

The Capricorn Cusp – January 21st to 23rd

What really sets you apart is a genuinely practical streak that isn't always present in the sign of Aquarius when taken alone. You are likely to have all the joy of life and much of the devil-may-care attitude of your Sun sign, but at the same time you are capable of getting things done in a very positive way. This makes you likely to achieve a higher degree of material success and means that you ally managerial skills with the potential for rolling up your sleeves and taking part in the 'real work' yourself. Alongside this you are able to harness the naturally intuitive qualities of Aquarius in a very matter-of-fact way. Few people would have the ability to pull the wool over your eyes and you are rarely stuck for a solution, even to apparently difficult problems.

You express yourself less well than Aquarius taken alone, and you may have a sort of reserve that leads others to believe that your mind is full of still waters which run very deep. The air of mystery can actually be quite useful, because it masks an ability to react and move quickly when necessary, which is a great surprise to the people around you. However, there are two sides to every coin and if there is a slightly negative quality to this cuspid position it might lie in the fact that you are not quite the communicator that tends to be the case with Aquarius, and you could go through some fairly quiet and introspective phases that those around you would find somewhat difficult to understand. In a positive sense this offers a fairly wistful aspect to your nature that may, in romantic applications, appear very attractive. There is something deeply magnetic about your nature and it isn't quite possible for everyone to understand what makes you tick. Actually this is part of your appeal because there is nothing like curiosity on the part of others to enhance your profile.

Getting things done is what matters the most to you, harnessed to the ability to see the wider picture in life. It's true that not everyone understands your complex nature, but in friendship you are scarcely short of supportive types. Family members can be especially important to you and personal attachments are invariably made for life.

The Pisces Cusp – February 17th to 19th

It appears that you are more of a thinker than most and achieve depths of contemplation that would be totally alien to some signs of the zodiac. Much of your life is given over to the service you show for humanity as a whole but you don't sink into the depths of despair in the way that some Piscean individuals are inclined to do. You are immensely likeable and rarely stuck for a good idea. You know how to enjoy yourself, even if this quality is usually tied to the support and assistance that you constantly give to those around you.

Many of you will already have chosen a profession that somehow fulfils your need to be of service, and it isn't unusual for Pisces-cusp Aquarians to alter their path in life totally if it isn't fulfilling this most basic requirement. When necessary, you can turn your hand to almost anything, generally giving yourself totally to the task in hand, sometimes to the exclusion of everything else. People with this combination often have two very different sorts of career, sometimes managing to do both at the same time. Confidence in practical matters isn't usually lacking, even if you sometimes think that your thought processes are a little bit muddled.

In love you are ardent and more sincere than Aquarius sometimes seems to be. There can be a tinge of jealousy at work now and again in deep relationships, but you are less likely than Pisces to let this show. You tend to be very protective of the people who are most important in your life and these are probably fewer in number than often seems to be the case for Aquarius. Your love of humanity and the needs it has of you are of supreme importance and you barely let a day pass without offering some sort of assistance. For this reason, and many others, you are a much loved individual and show your most caring face to the world for the majority of your life. Material success can be hard to come by at first, but it isn't really an aspect of life that worries you too much in any case. It is far more important for you to be content with your lot and, if you are happy, it seems that more or less everything else tends to follow.

AQUARIUS AND ITS ASCENDANTS

The nature of every individual on the planet is composed of the rich variety of zodiac signs and planetary positions that were present at the time of their birth. Your Sun sign, which in your case is Aquarius, is one of the many factors when it comes to assessing the unique person you are. Probably the most important consideration, other than your Sun sign, is to establish the zodiac sign that was rising over the eastern horizon at the time that you were born. This is your Ascending or Rising sign. Most popular astrology fails to take account of the Ascendant, and yet its importance remains with you from the very moment of your birth, through every day of your life. The Ascendant is evident in the way you approach the world, and so, when meeting a person for the first time, it is this astrological influence that you are most likely to notice first. Our Ascending sign essentially represents what we appear to be, while the Sun sign is what we feel inside ourselves.

The Ascendant also has the potential for modifying our overall nature. For example, if you were born at a time of day when Aquarius was passing over the eastern horizon (this would be around the time of dawn) then you would be classed as a double Aquarian. As such, you would typify this zodiac sign, both internally and in your dealings with others. However, if your Ascendant sign turned out to be a Fire sign, such as Aries, there would be a profound alteration of nature, away from the expected qualities of Aquarius.

One of the reasons why popular astrology often ignores the Ascendant is that it has always been rather difficult to establish. We have found a way to make this possible by devising an easy-to-use table, which you will find on page 157 of this book. Using this, you can establish your Ascendant sign at a glance. You will need to know your rough time of birth, then it is simply a case of following the instructions.

For those readers who have no idea of their time of birth it might be worth allowing a good friend, or perhaps your partner, to read through the section that follows this introduction. Someone who deals with you on a regular basis may easily discover your Ascending sign, even though you could have some difficulty establishing it for yourself. A good understanding of this component of your nature is essential if you want to be aware of that 'other person' who is responsible for the way you make contact with the world at large. Your Sun sign, Ascendant sign, and the other pointers in this book will, together, allow you a far better understanding of what makes you tick as an individual. Peeling back the different layers of your astrological make-up can be an enlightening experience, and the Ascendant may represent one of the most important layers of all.

Aquarius with Aquarius Ascendant

You are totally unique and quite original, so much so that very few people could claim to understand what makes you tick. Routines get on your nerves and you need to be out there doing something most of the time. Getting where you want to go in life isn't too difficult, except that when you arrive, your destination might not look half so interesting as it did before. You are well liked and should have many friends. This is not to say that your pals have much in common with each other, because you choose from a wide cross-section of people. Although folks see you as being very reasonable in the main, you are capable of being quite cranky on occasions. Your intuition is extremely strong and is far less likely to let you down than would be the case with some individuals.

Travel is very important to you and you will probably live for some time in a different part of your own country, or even in another part of the world. At work you are more than capable, but do need something to do that you find personally stimulating, because you are not very good at constant routine. You can be relied upon to use your originality and find solutions that are instinctive and brilliant. Most people are very fond of you.

Aquarius with Pisces Ascendant

Here we find the originality of Aquarius balanced by the very sensitive qualities of Pisces, and it makes for a very interesting combination. When it comes to understanding other people you are second to none, but it's certain that you are more instinctive than either Pisces or Aquarius when taken alone. You are better at routines than Aquarius, but also relish a challenge more than the typical Piscean would. Active and enterprising, you tend to know what you want from life, but consideration of others, and the world at large, will always be part of the scenario. People with this combination often work on behalf of humanity and are to be found in social work, the medical profession and religious institutions. As far as beliefs are concerned you don't conform to established patterns, and yet may get closer to the truth of the Creator than many deep theological thinkers have ever been able to do. Acting on impulse as much as you do means that not everyone understands the way your mind works, but your popularity will invariably see you through.

Passionate and deeply sensitive, you are able to negotiate the twists and turns of a romantic life that is hardly likely to be run-of-the-mill. In the end, however, you should be able to discover a very deep personal and spiritual happiness.

Aquarius with Aries Ascendant

If ever anyone could be accused of setting off immediately, but slowly, it has to be you. These are very contradictory signs and the differences will express themselves in a variety of ways. One thing is certain, you have tremendous tenacity and will see a job through patiently from beginning to end, without tiring on the way and ensuring that every detail is taken care of properly. This combination often brings good health and a great capacity for continuity, particularly in terms of the length of life. You are certainly not as argumentative as the typical Aries, but you do know how to get your own way, which is just as well because you are usually thinking on behalf of everyone else and not just on your own account.

At home you can relax, which is a blessing for Aries, though in fact you seldom choose to do so because you always have some project or other on the go. You probably enjoy knocking down and rebuilding walls, though this is a practical tendency and not responsive to relationships, in which you are ardent and sincere. Impetuosity is as close to your heart as is the case for any type of subject, though you certainly have the ability to appear patient and steady. But it's just a front, isn't it?

Aquarius with Taurus Ascendant

There is nothing that you fail to think about deeply and with great intensity. You are wise, honest and very scientific in your approach to life. Routines are necessary in life but you have most of them sorted out well in advance and so always have time to look at the next interesting fact. If you don't spend all your time watching documentaries on the television set, you make a good friend and love to socialise. Most of the great discoveries of the world were probably made by people with this sort of astrological combination, though your nature is rather 'odd' on occasions and so can be rather difficult for others to understand.

You may be most surprised when others tell you that you are eccentric, but you don't really mind too much because for half of the time you are not inhabiting the same world as the rest of us. Because you can be delightfully dotty you are probably much loved and cherished by your friends, of which there are likely to be many. Family members probably adore you too, and you can be guaranteed to entertain anyone with whom you come into contact. The only fly in the ointment is that you sometimes lose track of reality, whatever that might be, and fly high in your own atmosphere of rarefied possibilities.

Aquarius with Gemini Ascendant

If you were around in the 1960s there is every chance that you were the first to go around with flowers in your hair. You are unconventional, original, quirky and entertaining. Few people would fail to notice your presence and you take life as it comes, even though on most occasions you are firmly in the driving seat. It all probability you care very much about the planet on which you live and the people with whom you share it. Not everyone understands you, but that does not really matter, for you have more than enough communication skills to put your message across intact. You should avoid wearing yourself out by worrying about things that you cannot control, and you definitely gain from taking time out to meditate. However, whether or not you allow yourself that luxury remains to be seen.

If you are not the most communicative form of Gemini subject then you must come a close second. Despite this fact much of what you have to say makes real sense and you revel in the company of interesting, intelligent and stimulating people, whose opinions on a host of matters will add to your own considerations. You are a true original in every sense of the word and the mere fact of your presence in the world is bound to add to the enjoyment of life experienced by the many people with whom you make contact.

Aquarius with Cancer Ascendant

The truly original spark, for which the sign of Aquarius is famed, can only enhance the caring qualities of Cancer, and is also inclined to bring the Crab out of its shell to a much greater extent than would be the case with certain other zodiac combinations. Aquarius is a party animal and never arrives without something interesting to say, which is doubly the case when the reservoir of emotion and consideration that is Cancer is feeding the tap. Your nature can be rather confusing for even you to deal with, but you are inspirational, bright, charming and definitely fun to be around.

The Cancer element in your nature means that you care about your home and the people to whom you are related. You are also a good and loyal friend, who would keep attachments for much longer than could be expected for Aquarius alone. You love to travel and can be expected to make many journeys to far-off places during your life. Some attention will have to be paid to your health, because you are capable of burning up masses of nervous energy, often without getting the periods of rest and contemplation that are essential to the deeper qualities of the sign of Cancer. Nevertheless you have determination, resilience and a refreshing attitude that lifts the spirits of the people in your vicinity.

Aquarius with Leo Ascendant

All associations with Aquarius bring originality, and you are no exception. You aspire to do your best most of the time but manage to achieve your objectives in an infinitely amusing and entertaining way. Not that you set out to do so, because if you are an actor on the stage of life, it seems as though you are a natural one. There is nothing remotely pretentious about your breezy personality or your ability to occupy the centre of any stage. This analogy is quite appropriate because you probably like the theatre. Being in any situation when reality is suspended for a while suits you down to the ground, and in any case you may regularly ask yourself if you even recognise what reality is. Always asking questions, both of yourself and the world at large, you soldier on relentlessly, though not to the exclusion of having a good time on the way.

Keeping to tried and tested paths is not your way. You are a natural trailblazer who is full of good ideas and who has the energy to put them into practice. You care deeply for the people who play an important part in your life but are wise enough to allow them the space they need to develop their own personalities along the way. Most people like you, many love you, and one or two think that you really are the best thing since sliced bread.

Aquarius with Virgo Ascendant

How could anyone make the convention unconventional? Well, if anyone can manage, you can. There are great contradictions here, because on the one hand you always want to do the expected thing, but the Aquarian quality within your nature loves to surprise everyone on the way. If you don't always know what you are thinking or doing, it's a pretty safe bet that others won't either, so it's important on occasions really to stop and think. However this is not a pressing concern, because you tend to live a fairly happy life and muddle through no matter what. Other people tend to take to you well and it is likely that you will have many friends. You tend to be bright and cheerful and can approach even difficult tasks with the certainty that you have the skills necessary to see them through to their conclusion. Give and take are important factors in the life of any individual and particularly so in your case. Because you can stretch yourself in order to understand what makes other people think and act in the way that they do, you have the reputation of being a good friend and a reliable colleague.

In love you can be somewhat more fickle than the typical Virgoan, and yet you are always interesting to live with. Where you are, things happen, and you mix a sparkling wit with deep insights.

Aquarius with Libra Ascendant

Stand by for a truly interesting and very inspiring combination here, but one that is sometimes rather difficult to fathom, even for the sort of people who believe themselves to be very perceptive. The reason for this could be that any situation has to be essentially fixed and constant in order to get a handle on it, and this is certainly not the case for the Aquarian–Libran type. The fact is that both these signs are Air signs, and to a certain extent as unpredictable as the wind itself.

To most people you seem to be original, frank, free and very outspoken. Not everything you do makes sense to others and if you were alive during the hippy era, it is likely that you went around with flowers in your hair, for you are a free-thinking idealist at heart. With age you mature somewhat, but never too much, because you will always see the strange, the comical and the original in life. This is what keeps you young and is one of the factors that makes you so very attractive to members of the opposite sex. Many people will want to 'adopt' you and you are at your very best when in company. Much of your effort is expounded on others and yet, unless you discipline yourself a good deal, personal relationships of the romantic sort can bring certain difficulties. Careful planning is necessary.

Aquarius with Scorpio Ascendant

Here we have a combination that shows much promise and a flexibility that allows many changes in direction, allied to a power to succeed, sometimes very much against all the odds. Aquarius lightens the load of the Scorpio mind, turning the depths into potential, and intuitive foresight into a means for getting on in life. There are depths here, because even airy Aquarius isn't so easy to understand, and it is therefore a fact that some people with this combination will always be something of a mystery. However, even this fact can be turned to your advantage because it means that people will always be looking at you. Confidence is so often the key to success in life and the Scorpio–Aquarius mix offers this, or at least appears to do so. Even when this is not entirely the case, the fact that everyone around you believes it to be true is often enough.

You are usually good to know, and show a keen intellect and a deep intelligence, aided by a fascination for life that knows no bounds. When at your best you are giving, understanding, balanced and active. On those occasions when things are not going well for you, beware of a stubborn streak and the need to be sensational. Keep it light and happy and you won't go far wrong. Most of you are very, very much loved.

Aquarius with Sagittarius Ascendant

There is an original streak to your nature which is very attractive to the people with whom you share your life. Always different, ever on the go and anxious to try out the next experiment in life, you are interested in almost everything, and yet deeply attached to almost nothing. Everyone you know thinks that you are a little 'odd', but you probably don't mind them believing this because you know it to be true. In fact it is possible that you positively relish your eccentricity, which sets you apart from the common herd and means that you are always going to be noticed.

Although it may seem strange with this combination of Air and Fire, you can be distinctly cool on occasions, have a deep and abiding love of your own company now and again and won't be easily understood. Love comes fairly easily to you but there are times when you are accused of being self-possessed, self-indulgent and not willing enough to fall in line with the wishes of those around you. Despite this you walk on and on down your own path. At heart you are an extrovert and you love to party, often late into the night. Luxury appeals to you, though it tends to be of the transient sort. Travel could easily play a major and a very important part in your life.

Aquarius with Capricorn Ascendant

Here the determination of Capricorn is assisted by a slightly more adaptable quality and an off-beat personality that tends to keep everyone else guessing. You don't care to be quite so predictable as the archetypal Capricorn would be, and there is a more idealistic quality here, or at least one that shows more. A greater number of friends than Capricorn usually keeps is likely, though less than the true Aquarian would gather. Few people doubt your sincerity, though by no means all of them understand what makes you tick. Unfortunately you are not in a position to help them out, because you are not too sure yourself. All the same, you muddle through and can be very capable when the mood takes you.

Being a natural traveller, you love to see new places and would be quite fascinated by cultures that are very different to your own. People with this combination are inclined to spend some time living abroad and may even settle there. You look out for the underdog and will always have time for a good cause, no matter what it takes to help. In romantic terms you are a reliable partner, though with a slightly wayward edge which, if anything, tends to make you even more attractive. Listen to your intuition, which is well honed and rarely lets you down. Generally speaking you are very popular.

THE MOON AND THE PART IT PLAYS IN YOUR LIFE

In astrology the Moon is probably the single most important heavenly body after the Sun. Its unique position, as partner to the Earth on its journey around the solar system, means that the Moon appears to pass through the signs of the zodiac extremely quickly. The zodiac position of the Moon at the time of your birth plays a great part in personal character and is especially significant in the build-up of your emotional nature.

Your Own Moon Sign

Discovering the position of the Moon at the time of your birth has always been notoriously difficult because tracking the complex zodiac positions of the Moon is not easy. This process has been reduced to three simple stages with our Lunar Tables. A breakdown of the Moon's zodiac positions can be found from page 35 onwards, so that once you know what your Moon Sign is, you can see what part this plays in the overall build-up of your personal character.

If you follow the instructions on the next page you will soon be able to work out exactly what zodiac sign the Moon occupied on the day that you were born and you can then go on to compare the reading for this position with those of your Sun sign and your Ascendant. It is partly the comparison between these three important positions that goes towards making you the unique individual you are.

HOW TO DISCOVER YOUR MOON SIGN

This is a three-stage process. You may need a pen and a piece of paper but if you follow the instructions below the process should only take a minute or so.

STAGE 1 First of all you need to know the Moon Age at the time of your birth. If you look at Moon Table 1, on page 33, you will find all the years between 1920 and 2018 down the left side. Find the year of your birth and then trace across to the right to the month of your birth. Where the two intersect you will find a number. This is the date of the New Moon in the month that you were born. You now need to count forward the number of days between the New Moon and your own birthday. For example, if the New Moon in the month of your birth was shown as being the 6th and you were born on the 20th, your Moon Age Day would be 14. If the New Moon in the month of your birth came after your birthday, you need to count forward from the New Moon in the previous month, which, if you were born in January, means you must look at December in the previous year. You cannot count from December in the year of your birth, as that month is *after* your birth. Whatever the result, jot this number down so that you do not forget it.

STAGE 2 Take a look at Moon Table 2 on page 34. Down the left hand column look for the date of your birth. Now trace across to the month of your birth. Where the two meet you will find a letter. Copy this letter down alongside your Moon Age Day.

STAGE 3 Moon Table 3 on page 34 will supply you with the zodiac sign the Moon occupied on the day of your birth. Look for your Moon Age Day down the left hand column and then for the letter you found in Stage 2. Where the two converge you will find a zodiac sign and this is the sign occupied by the Moon on the day that you were born.

Your Zodiac Moon Sign Explained

You will find a profile of all zodiac Moon Signs on pages 35 to 38, showing in yet another way how astrology helps to make you into the individual that you are. In each daily entry of the Astral Diary you can find the zodiac position of the Moon for every day of the year. This also allows you to discover your lunar birthdays. Since the Moon passes through all the signs of the zodiac in about a month, you can expect something like twelve lunar birthdays each year. At these times you are likely to be emotionally steady and able to make the sort of decisions that have real, lasting value.

MOON TABLE 1

YEAR	DEC	JAN	FEB	YEAR	DEC	JAN	FEB	YEAR	DEC	JAN	FEB
1920	10	20	19	1953	6	15	14	1986	1/30	10	9
1921	29	9	8	1954	25	5	3	1987	20	29	28
1922	18	27	26	1955	14	24	22	1988	9	19	17
1923	8	17	15	1956	2	13	11	1989	28	7	6
1924	26	6	5	1957	21	1/30	–	1990	17	26	25
1925	15	24	23	1958	10	19	18	1991	6	15	14
1926	5	14	12	1959	29	9	7	1992	24	4	3
1927	24	3	2	1960	18	27	26	1993	14	23	22
1928	12	21	19	1961	7	16	15	1994	2	11	10
1929	1/30	11	9	1962	26	6	5	1995	22	1/30	–
1930	19	29	28	1963	15	25	23	1996	10	20	18
1931	9	18	17	1964	4	14	13	1997	28	9	7
1932	27	7	6	1965	22	3	1	1998	18	27	26
1933	17	25	24	1966	12	21	19	1999	7	17	16
1934	6	15	14	1967	1/30	10	9	2000	26	6	4
1935	25	5	3	1968	20	29	28	2001	15	25	23
1936	13	24	22	1969	9	19	17	2002	4	13	12
1937	2	12	11	1970	28	7	6	2003	23	3	1
1938	21	1/31	–	1971	17	26	25	2004	11	21	20
1939	10	20	19	1972	6	15	14	2005	30	10	9
1940	28	9	8	1973	25	5	4	2006	20	29	28
1941	18	27	26	1974	14	24	22	2007	9	18	16
1942	8	16	15	1975	3	12	11	2008	27	8	6
1943	27	6	4	1976	21	1/31	29	2009	16	26	25
1944	15	25	24	1977	10	19	18	2010	6	15	14
1945	4	14	12	1978	29	9	7	2011	25	4	3
1946	23	3	2	1979	18	27	26	2012	12	23	22
1947	12	21	19	1980	7	16	15	2013	2	12	10
1948	1/30	11	9	1981	26	6	4	2014	2	1/31	–
1949	19	29	27	1982	15	25	23	2015	20	19	20
1950	9	18	16	1983	4	14	13	2016	29	9	8
1951	28	7	6	1984	22	3	1	2017	18	27	25
1952	17	26	25	1985	12	21	19	2018	7	16	15

TABLE 2

DAY	JAN	FEB
1	A	D
2	A	D
3	A	D
4	A	D
5	A	D
6	A	D
7	A	D
8	A	D
9	A	D
10	A	E
11	B	E
12	B	E
13	B	E
14	B	E
15	B	E
16	B	E
17	B	E
18	B	E
19	B	E
20	B	F
21	C	F
22	C	F
23	C	F
24	C	F
25	C	F
26	C	F
27	C	F
28	C	F
29	C	F
30	C	–
31	D	–

MOON TABLE 3

M/D	A	B	C	D	E	F	G
0	CP	AQ	AQ	AQ	PI	PI	PI
1	AQ	AQ	AQ	PI	PI	PI	AR
2	AQ	AQ	PI	PI	PI	AR	AR
3	AQ	PI	PI	PI	AR	AR	AR
4	PI	PI	AR	AR	AR	AR	TA
5	PI	AR	AR	AR	TA	TA	TA
6	AR	AR	AR	TA	TA	TA	GE
7	AR	AR	TA	TA	TA	GE	GE
8	AR	TA	TA	TA	GE	GE	GE
9	TA	TA	GE	GE	GE	CA	CA
10	TA	GE	GE	GE	CA	CA	CA
11	GE	GE	GE	CA	CA	CA	LE
12	GE	GE	CA	CA	CA	LE	LE
13	GE	CA	CA	LE	LE	LE	LE
14	CA	CA	LE	LE	LE	VI	VI
15	CA	LE	LE	LE	VI	VI	VI
16	LE	LE	LE	VI	VI	VI	LI
17	LE	LE	VI	VI	VI	LI	LI
18	LE	VI	VI	VI	LI	LI	LI
19	VI	VI	VI	LI	LI	LI	SC
20	VI	LI	LI	LI	SC	SC	SC
21	LI	LI	LI	SC	SC	SC	SA
22	LI	LI	SC	SC	SC	SA	SA
23	LI	SC	SC	SC	SA	SA	SA
24	SC	SC	SC	SA	SA	SA	CP
25	SC	SA	SA	SA	CP	CP	CP
26	SA	SA	SA	CP	CP	CP	AQ
27	SA	SA	CP	CP	AQ	AQ	AQ
28	SA	CP	CP	AQ	AQ	AQ	AQ
29	CP	CP	CP	AQ	AQ	AQ	PI

AR = Aries, TA = Taurus, GE = Gemini, CA = Cancer, LE = Leo, VI = Virgo,
LI = Libra, SC = Scorpio, SA = Sagittarius, CP = Capricorn, AQ = Aquarius, PI = Pisces

MOON SIGNS

Moon in Aries

You have a strong imagination, courage, determination and a desire to do things in your own way and forge your own path through life.

Originality is a key attribute; you are seldom stuck for ideas although your mind is changeable and you could take the time to focus on individual tasks. Often quick-tempered, you take orders from few people and live life at a fast pace. Avoid health problems by taking regular time out for rest and relaxation.

Emotionally, it is important that you talk to those you are closest to and work out your true feelings. Once you discover that people are there to help, there is less necessity for you to do everything yourself.

Moon in Taurus

The Moon in Taurus gives you a courteous and friendly manner, which means you are likely to have many friends.

The good things in life mean a lot to you, as Taurus is an Earth sign that delights in experiences which please the senses. Hence you are probably a lover of good food and drink, which may in turn mean you need to keep an eye on the bathroom scales, especially as looking good is also important to you.

Emotionally you are fairly stable and you stick by your own standards. Taureans do not respond well to change. Intuition also plays an important part in your life.

Moon in Gemini

You have a warm-hearted character, sympathetic and eager to help others. At times reserved, you can also be articulate and chatty: this is part of the paradox of Gemini, which always brings duplicity to the nature. You are interested in current affairs, have a good intellect, and are good company and likely to have many friends. Most of your friends have a high opinion of you and would be ready to defend you should the need arise. However, this is usually unnecessary, as you are quite capable of defending yourself in any verbal confrontation.

Travel is important to your inquisitive mind and you find intellectual stimulus in mixing with people from different cultures. You also gain much from reading, writing and the arts but you do need plenty of rest and relaxation in order to avoid fatigue.

Moon in Cancer

The Moon in Cancer at the time of birth is a fortunate position as Cancer is the Moon's natural home. This means that the qualities of compassion and understanding given by the Moon are especially enhanced in your nature, and you are friendly and sociable and cope well with emotional pressures. You cherish home and family life, and happily do the domestic tasks. Your surroundings are important to you and you hate squalor and filth. You are likely to have a love of music and poetry.

Your basic character, although at times changeable like the Moon itself, depends on symmetry. You aim to make your surroundings comfortable and harmonious, for yourself and those close to you.

Moon in Leo

The best qualities of the Moon and Leo come together to make you warm-hearted, fair, ambitious and self-confident. With good organisational abilities, you invariably rise to a position of responsibility in your chosen career. This is fortunate as you don't enjoy being an 'also-ran' and would rather be an important part of a small organisation than a menial in a large one.

You should be lucky in love, and happy, provided you put in the effort to make a comfortable home for yourself and those close to you. It is likely that you will have a love of pleasure, sport, music and literature. Life brings you many rewards, most of them as a direct result of your own efforts, although you may be luckier than average and ready to make the best of any situation.

Moon in Virgo

You are endowed with good mental abilities and a keen receptive memory, but you are never ostentatious or pretentious. Naturally quite reserved, you still have many friends, especially of the opposite sex. Marital relationships must be discussed carefully and worked at so that they remain harmonious, as personal attachments can be a problem if you do not give them your full attention.

Talented and persevering, you possess artistic qualities and are a good homemaker. Earning your honours through genuine merit, you work long and hard towards your objectives but show little pride in your achievements. Many short journeys will be undertaken in your life.

Moon in Libra

With the Moon in Libra you are naturally popular and make friends easily. People like you, probably more than you realise, you bring fun to a party and are a natural diplomat. For all its good points, Libra is not the most stable of astrological signs and, as a result, your emotions can be a little unstable too. Therefore, although the Moon in Libra is said to be good for love and marriage, your Sun sign and Rising sign will have an important effect on your emotional and loving qualities.

You must remember to relate to others in your decision-making. Co-operation is crucial because Libra represents the 'balance' of life that can only be achieved through harmonious relationships. Conformity is not easy for you because Libra, an Air sign, likes its independence.

Moon in Scorpio

Some people might call you pushy. In fact, all you really want to do is to live life to the full and protect yourself and your family from the pressures of life. Take care to avoid giving the impression of being sarcastic or impulsive and use your energies wisely and constructively.

You have great courage and you invariably achieve your goals by force of personality and sheer effort. You are fond of mystery and are good at predicting the outcome of situations and events. Travel experiences can be beneficial to you.

You may experience problems if you do not take time to examine your motives in a relationship, and also if you allow jealousy, always a feature of Scorpio, to cloud your judgement.

Moon in Sagittarius

The Moon in Sagittarius helps to make you a generous individual with humanitarian qualities and a kind heart. Restlessness may be intrinsic as your mind is seldom still. Perhaps because of this, you have a need for change that could lead you to several major moves during your adult life. You are not afraid to stand your ground when you know your judgement is right, you speak directly and have good intuition.

At work you are quick, efficient and versatile and so you make an ideal employee. You need work to be intellectually demanding and do not enjoy tedious routines.

In relationships, you anger quickly if faced with stupidity or deception, though you are just as quick to forgive and forget. Emotionally, there are times when your heart rules your head.

Moon in Capricorn

The Moon in Capricorn makes you popular and likely to come into the public eye in some way. The watery Moon is not entirely comfortable in the Earth sign of Capricorn and this may lead to some difficulties in the early years of life. An initial lack of creative ability and indecision must be overcome before the true qualities of patience and perseverance inherent in Capricorn can show through.

You have good administrative ability and are a capable worker, and if you are careful you can accumulate wealth. But you must be cautious and take professional advice in partnerships, as you are open to deception. You may be interested in social or welfare work, which suit your organisational skills and sympathy for others.

Moon in Aquarius

The Moon in Aquarius makes you an active and agreeable person with a friendly, easy-going nature. Sympathetic to the needs of others, you flourish in a laid-back atmosphere. You are broad-minded, fair and open to suggestion, although sometimes you have an unconventional quality which others can find hard to understand.

You are interested in the strange and curious, and in old articles and places. You enjoy trips to these places and gain much from them. Political, scientific and educational work interests you and you might choose a career in science or technology.

Money-wise, you make gains through innovation and concentration and Lunar Aquarians often tackle more than one job at a time. In love you are kind and honest.

Moon in Pisces

You have a kind, sympathetic nature, somewhat retiring at times, but you always take account of others' feelings and help when you can.

Personal relationships may be problematic, but as life goes on you can learn from your experiences and develop a better understanding of yourself and the world around you.

You have a fondness for travel, appreciate beauty and harmony and hate disorder and strife. You may be fond of literature and would make a good writer or speaker yourself. You have a creative imagination and may come across as an incurable romantic. You have strong intuition, maybe bordering on a mediumistic quality, which sets you apart from the mass. You may not be rich in cash terms, but your personal gifts are worth more than gold.

AQUARIUS IN LOVE

Discover how compatible in love you are with people from the same and other signs of the zodiac. Five stars equals a match made in heaven!

Aquarius meets Aquarius

This is a good match for several reasons. Most importantly, although it sounds arrogant, Aquarians like themselves. At its best, Aquarius is one of the fairest, most caring and genuinely pleasant zodiac signs and so it is only when faced by the difficulties created by others that it shows a less favourable side. Put two Aquarians together and voilà – instant success! Personal and family life should bring more joy. On the whole, a platform for adventure based on solid foundations. Star rating: *****

Aquarius meets Pisces

Zodiac signs that follow each other often have something in common, but this is not the case with Aquarius and Pisces. Both signs are deeply caring, but in different ways. Pisces is one of the deepest zodiac signs, and Aquarius simply isn't prepared to embark on the journey. Pisceans, meanwhile, would probably find Aquarians superficial and even flippant. On the positive side there is potential for a well-balanced relationship, but unless one party is untypical of their zodiac sign, it often doesn't get started. Star rating: **

Aquarius meets Aries

Aquarius is an Air sign, and Air and Fire often work well together, but not in the case of Aries and Aquarius. The average Aquarian lives in what the Ram sees as a fantasy world, so a meeting of minds is unlikely. Of course, the dominant side of Aries could be trained by the devil-may-care attitude of Aquarius. There are meeting points but they are difficult to establish. However, given sufficient time and an open mind on both sides, a degree of happiness is possible. Star rating: **

Aquarius meets Taurus

In any relationship of which Aquarius is a part, surprises abound. It is difficult for Taurus to understand the soul-searching, adventurous, changeable Aquarian, but on the positive side, the Bull is adaptable and can respond well to a dose of excitement. Aquarians are kind and react well to the same quality coming back at them. Both are friendly, capable of deep affection and basically creative. Unfortunately, Taurus simply doesn't know what makes Aquarius tick, which could lead to feelings of isolation, even if these don't always show on the surface. Star rating: **

Aquarius meets Gemini

Aquarius is commonly mistaken for a Water sign, but in fact it's ruled by the Air element, and this is the key to its compatibility with Gemini. Both signs mix freely socially, and each has an insatiable curiosity. There is plenty of action, lots of love, but very little rest, and so great potential for success if they don't wear each other out! Aquarius revels in its own eccentricity, and encourages Gemini to emulate this. Theirs will be an unconventional household, but almost everyone warms to this crazy and unpredictable couple. Star rating: *****

Aquarius meets Cancer

Cancer is often attracted to Aquarius and, as Aquarius is automatically on the side of anyone who fancies it, so there is the potential for something good here. Cancer loves Aquarius' devil-may-care approach to life, but also recognises and seeks to strengthen the basic lack of self-confidence that all Air signs try so hard to keep secret. Both signs are natural travellers and are quite adventurous. Their family life could be unusual, but friends would recognise a caring, sharing household with many different interests shared by people genuinely in love. Star rating: ***

Aquarius meets Leo

The problem here is that Aquarius doesn't think in the general sense of the word, it knows. Leo, on the other hand, is more practical and relies more on logical reasoning, and consequently it doesn't understand Aquarius very well. Aquarians can also appear slightly frosty in their appreciation of others and this, too, will annoy Leo. This is a good match for a business partnership because Aquarius is astute, while Leo is brave, but personally the prognosis is less promising. Tolerance, understanding and forbearance are all needed to make this work. Star rating: **

Aquarius meets Virgo

Aquarius is a strange sign because no matter how well one knows it, it always manages to surprise. For this reason, against the odds, it's quite likely that Aquarius will form a successful relationship with Virgo. Aquarius is changeable, unpredictable and often quite odd, while Virgo is steady, a fuss-pot and very practical. Herein lies the key. What one sign needs, the other provides and that may be the surest recipe for success imaginable. On-lookers may not know why the couple are happy, but they will recognise that this is the case. Star rating: ****

Aquarius meets Libra

One of the best combinations imaginable, partly because both are Air signs and so share a common meeting point. But perhaps the more crucial factor is that both signs respect each other. Aquarius loves life and originality, and is quite intellectual. Libra is similar, but more balanced and rather less eccentric. A visit to this couple's house would be entertaining and full of zany wit, activity and excitement. Both are keen to travel and may prefer to 'find themselves' before taking on too many domestic responsibilities. Star rating: *****

Aquarius meets Scorpio

This is a promising and practical combination. Scorpio responds well to Aquarius' persistent exploration of its deep nature and so this generally shy sign becomes lighter, brighter and more inspirational. Meanwhile, Aquarians are rarely as sure of themselves as they like to appear and are reassured by Scorpio's constant, steady and determined support. Both signs want to be kind to each other, which is a good starting point to a relationship that should be warm most of the time and extremely hot occasionally. Star rating: ****

Aquarius meets Sagittarius

Both Sagittarius and Aquarius are into mind games, which may lead to something of an intellectual competition. If one side is happy to be 'bamboozled' it won't be a problem, but it is more likely that the relationship will turn into a competition, which won't auger well for its long-term future. However, on the plus side, both signs are adventurous and sociable, so as long as there is always something new and interesting to do, the match could turn out very well. Star rating: **

Aquarius meets Capricorn

Probably one of the least likely combinations, as Capricorn and Aquarius are unlikely to choose each other in the first place, unless one side is quite untypical of their sign. Capricorn approaches things in a practical way and likes to get things done, while Aquarius works almost exclusively for the moment and relies heavily on intuition. Their attitudes to romance are also diametrically opposed: Aquarius' moods tend to swing from red hot to ice cold in a minute, which is alien to steady Capricorn. Star rating: **

VENUS:
THE PLANET OF LOVE

If you look up at the sky around sunset or sunrise you will often see Venus in close attendance to the Sun. It is arguably one of the most beautiful sights of all and there is little wonder that historically it became associated with the goddess of love. But although Venus does play an important part in the way you view love and in the way others see you romantically, this is only one of the spheres of influence that it enjoys in your overall character.

Venus has a part to play in the more cultured side of your life and has much to do with your appreciation of art, literature, music and general creativity. Even the way you look is responsive to the part of the zodiac that Venus occupied at the start of your life, though this fact is also down to your Sun sign and Ascending sign. If, at the time you were born, Venus occupied one of the more gregarious zodiac signs, you will be more likely to wear your heart on your sleeve, as well as to be more attracted to entertainment, social gatherings and good company. If on the other hand Venus occupied a quiet zodiac sign at the time of your birth, you would tend to be more retiring and less willing to shine in public situations.

It's good to know what part the planet Venus plays in your life for it can have a great bearing on the way you appear to the rest of the world and since we all have to mix with others, you can learn to make the very best of what Venus has to offer you.

One of the great complications in the past has always been trying to establish exactly what zodiac position Venus enjoyed when you were born because the planet is notoriously difficult to track. However, we have solved that problem by creating a table that is exclusive to your Sun sign, which you will find on the following page.

Establishing your Venus sign could not be easier. Just look up the year of your birth on the following page and you will see a sign of the zodiac. This was the sign that Venus occupied in the period covered by your sign in that year. If Venus occupied more than one sign during the period, this is indicated by the date on which the sign changed, and the name of the new sign. For instance, if you were born in 1945, Venus was in Pisces until the 12th February, after which time it was in Aries. If you were born before 12th February your Venus sign is Pisces, if you were born on or after 12th February, your Venus sign is Aries. Once you have established the position of Venus at the time of your birth, you can then look in the pages which follow to see how this has a bearing on your life as a whole.

43

1920 SAGITTARIUS / 30.1 CAPRICORN
1921 PISCES / 15.2 ARIES
1922 CAPRICORN / 25.1 AQUARIUS / 18.2 PISCES
1923 SAGITTARIUS / 7.2 CAPRICORN
1924 PISCES / 13.2 ARIES
1925 CAPRICORN / 9.2 AQUARIUS
1926 AQUARIUS
1927 AQUARIUS / 2.2 PISCES
1928 SAGITTARIUS / 29.1 CAPRICORN
1929 PISCES / 14.2 ARIES
1930 CAPRICORN / 25.1 AQUARIUS / 18.2 PISCES
1931 SAGITTARIUS / 6.2 CAPRICORN
1932 PISCES / 13.2 ARIES
1933 CAPRICORN / 8.2 AQUARIUS
1934 AQUARIUS
1935 AQUARIUS / 2.2 PISCES
1936 SAGITTARIUS / 29.1 CAPRICORN
1937 PISCES / 13.2 ARIES
1938 CAPRICORN / 24.1 AQUARIUS / 17.2 PISCES
1939 SAGITTARIUS / 6.2 CAPRICORN
1940 PISCES / 12.2 ARIES
1941 CAPRICORN / 8.2 AQUARIUS
1942 AQUARIUS
1943 AQUARIUS / 1.2 PISCES
1944 SAGITTARIUS / 28.1 CAPRICORN
1945 PISCES / 12.2 ARIES
1946 CAPRICORN / 24.1 AQUARIUS / 17.2 PISCES
1947 SAGITTARIUS / 6.2 CAPRICORN
1948 PISCES / 12.2 ARIES
1949 CAPRICORN / 7.2 AQUARIUS
1950 AQUARIUS
1951 AQUARIUS / 1.2 PISCES
1952 SAGITTARIUS / 27.1 CAPRICORN
1953 PISCES / 11.2 ARIES
1954 CAPRICORN / 23.1 AQUARIUS / 16.2 PISCES
1955 SAGITTARIUS / 6.2 CAPRICORN
1956 PISCES / 11.2 ARIES
1957 CAPRICORN / 7.2 AQUARIUS
1958 AQUARIUS
1959 AQUARIUS / 31.1 PISCES
1960 SAGITTARIUS / 27.1 CAPRICORN
1961 PISCES / 9.2 ARIES
1962 CAPRICORN / 23.1 AQUARIUS / 15.2 PISCES
1963 SAGITTARIUS / 6.2 CAPRICORN
1964 PISCES / 11.2 ARIES
1965 CAPRICORN / 6.2 AQUARIUS
1966 AQUARIUS
1967 AQUARIUS / 30.1 PISCES

1968 SAGITTARIUS / 26.1 CAPRICORN
1969 PISCES / 7.2 ARIES
1970 CAPRICORN / 22.1 AQUARIUS / 15.2 PISCES
1971 SAGITTARIUS / 5.2 CAPRICORN
1972 PISCES / 10.2 ARIES
1973 CAPRICORN / 5.2 AQUARIUS
1974 AQUARIUS / 7.2 CAPRICORN
1975 AQUARIUS / 30.1 PISCES
1976 SAGITTARIUS / 26.1 CAPRICORN
1977 PISCES / 5.2 ARIES
1978 CAPRICORN / 22.1 AQUARIUS / 14.2 PISCES
1979 SAGITTARIUS / 5.2 CAPRICORN
1980 PISCES / 10.2 ARIES
1981 CAPRICORN / 5.2 AQUARIUS
1982 AQUARIUS / 29.1 CAPRICORN
1983 AQUARIUS / 29.1 PISCES
1984 SAGITTARIUS / 25.1 CAPRICORN
1985 PISCES / 5.2 ARIES
1986 AQUARIUS / 14.2 PISCES
1987 SAGITTARIUS / 5.2 CAPRICORN
1988 PISCES / 9.2 ARIES
1989 CAPRICORN / 4.2 AQUARIUS
1990 AQUARIUS / 23.1 CAPRICORN
1991 AQUARIUS / 29.1 PISCES
1992 SAGITTARIUS / 25.1 CAPRICORN
1993 PISCES / 4.2 ARIES
1994 AQUARIUS / 13.2 PISCES
1995 SAGITTARIUS / 5.2 CAPRICORN
1996 PISCES / 9.2 ARIES
1997 CAPRICORN / 4.2 AQUARIUS
1998 AQUARIUS / 23.1 CAPRICORN
1999 AQUARIUS / 29.1 PISCES
2000 SAGITTARIUS / 25.1 CAPRICORN
2001 PISCES / 4.2 ARIES
2002 AQUARIUS / 13.2 PISCES
2003 SAGITTARIUS
2004 PISCES / 9.2 AQUARIUS
2005 CAPRICORN / 6.2 AQUARIUS
2006 AQUARIUS / 14.01 CAPRICORN
2007 AQUARIUS / 19.01 PISCES
2008 SAGITTARIUS / 25.1 CAPRICORN
2009 PISCES / 4.2 ARIES
2010 AQUARIUS / 12.2 PISCES
2011 SAGITTARIUS
2012 PISCES / 9.2 AQUARIUS
2013 CAPRICORN / 6.2 AQUARIUS
2014 CAPRICORN / 6.2 AQUARIUS
2015 AQUARIUS / 29.1 PISCES
2016 SAGITTARIUS / 24.1 AQUARIUS
2017 PISCES / 4.2 ARIES
2018 AQUARIUS / 12.2 PISCES

VENUS THROUGH THE ZODIAC SIGNS

Venus in Aries

Amongst other things, the position of Venus in Aries indicates a fondness for travel, music and all creative pursuits. Your nature tends to be affectionate and you would try not to create confusion or difficulty for others if it could be avoided. Many people with this planetary position have a great love of the theatre, and mental stimulation is of the greatest importance. Early romantic attachments are common with Venus in Aries, so it is very important to establish a genuine sense of romantic continuity. Early marriage is not recommended, especially if it is based on sympathy. You may give your heart a little too readily on occasions.

Venus in Taurus

You are capable of very deep feelings and your emotions tend to last for a very long time. This makes you a trusting partner and lover, whose constancy is second to none. In life you are precise and careful and always try to do things the right way. Although this means an ordered life, which you are comfortable with, it can also lead you to be rather too fussy for your own good. Despite your pleasant nature, you are very fixed in your opinions and quite able to speak your mind. Others are attracted to you and historical astrologers always quoted this position of Venus as being very fortunate in terms of marriage. However, if you find yourself involved in a failed relationship, it could take you a long time to trust again.

Venus in Gemini

As with all associations related to Gemini, you tend to be quite versatile, anxious for change and intelligent in your dealings with the world at large. You may gain money from more than one source but you are equally good at spending it. There is an inference here that you are a good communicator, via either the written or the spoken word, and you love to be in the company of interesting people. Always on the look-out for culture, you may also be very fond of music, and love to indulge the curious and cultured side of your nature. In romance you tend to have more than one relationship and could find yourself associated with someone who has previously been a friend or even a distant relative.

Venus in Cancer

You often stay close to home because you are very fond of family and enjoy many of your most treasured moments when you are with those you love. Being naturally sympathetic, you will always do anything you can to support those around you, even people you hardly know at all. This charitable side of your nature is your most noticeable trait and is one of the reasons why others are naturally so fond of you. Being receptive and in some cases even psychic, you can see through to the soul of most of those with whom you come into contact. You may not commence too many romantic attachments but when you do give your heart, it tends to be unconditionally.

Venus in Leo

It must become quickly obvious to almost anyone you meet that you are kind, sympathetic and yet determined enough to stand up for anyone or anything that is truly important to you. Bright and sunny, you warm the world with your natural enthusiasm and would rarely do anything to hurt those around you, or at least not intentionally. In romance you are ardent and sincere, though some may find your style just a little overpowering. Gains come through your contacts with other people and this could be especially true with regard to romance, for love and money often come hand in hand for those who were born with Venus in Leo. People claim to understand you, though you are more complex than you seem.

Venus in Virgo

Your nature could well be fairly quiet no matter what your Sun sign might be, though this fact often manifests itself as an inner peace and would not prevent you from being basically sociable. Some delays and even the odd disappointment in love cannot be ruled out with this planetary position, though it's a fact that you will usually find the happiness you look for in the end. Catapulting yourself into romantic entanglements that you know to be rather ill-advised is not sensible, and it would be better to wait before you committed yourself exclusively to any one person. It is the essence of your nature to serve the world at large and through doing so it is possible that you will attract money at some stage in your life.

Venus in Libra

Venus is very comfortable in Libra and bestows upon those people who have this planetary position a particular sort of kindness that is easy to recognise. This is a very good position for all sorts of friendships and also for romantic attachments that usually bring much joy into your life. Few individuals with Venus in Libra would avoid marriage and since you are capable of great depths of love, it is likely that you will find a contented personal life. You like to mix with people of integrity and intelligence but don't take kindly to scruffy surroundings or work that means getting your hands too dirty. Careful speculation, good business dealings and money through marriage all seem fairly likely.

Venus in Scorpio

You are quite open and tend to spend money quite freely, even on those occasions when you don't have very much. Although your intentions are always good, there are times when you get yourself in to the odd scrape and this can be particularly true when it comes to romance, which you may come to late or from a rather unexpected direction. Certainly you have the power to be happy and to make others contented on the way, but you find the odd stumbling block on your journey through life and it could seem that you have to work harder than those around you. As a result of this, you gain a much deeper understanding of the true value of personal happiness than many people ever do, and are likely to achieve true contentment in the end.

Venus in Sagittarius

You are lighthearted, cheerful and always able to see the funny side of any situation. These facts enhance your popularity, which is especially high with members of the opposite sex. You should never have to look too far to find romantic interest in your life, though it is just possible that you might be too willing to commit yourself before you are certain that the person in question is right for you. Part of the problem here extends to other areas of life too. The fact is that you like variety in everything and so can tire of situations that fail to offer it. All the same, if you choose wisely and learn to understand your restless side, then great happiness can be yours.

Venus in Capricorn

The most notable trait that comes from Venus in this position is that it makes you trustworthy and able to take on all sorts of responsibilities in life. People are instinctively fond of you and love you all the more because you are always ready to help those who are in any form of need. Social and business popularity can be yours and there is a magnetic quality to your nature that is particularly attractive in a romantic sense. Anyone who wants a partner for a lover, a spouse and a good friend too would almost certainly look in your direction. Constancy is the hallmark of your nature and unfaithfulness would go right against the grain. You might sometimes be a little too trusting.

Venus in Aquarius

This location of Venus offers a fondness for travel and a desire to try out something new at every possible opportunity. You are extremely easy to get along with and tend to have many friends from varied backgrounds, classes and inclinations. You like to live a distinct sort of life and gain a great deal from moving about, both in a career sense and with regard to your home. It is not out of the question that you could form a romantic attachment to someone who comes from far away or be attracted to a person of a distinctly artistic and original nature. What you cannot stand is jealousy, for you have friends of both sexes and would want to keep things that way.

Venus in Pisces

The first thing people tend to notice about you is your wonderful, warm smile. Being very charitable by nature you will do anything to help others, even if you don't know them well. Much of your life may be spent sorting out situations for other people, but it is very important to feel that you are living for yourself too. In the main, you remain cheerful, and tend to be quite attractive to members of the opposite sex. Where romantic attachments are concerned, you could be drawn to people who are significantly older or younger than yourself or to someone with a unique career or point of view. It might be best for you to avoid marrying whilst you are still very young.

AQUARIUS:
2017 DIARY PAGES

October 2017

1 SUNDAY
Moon Age Day 11   Moon Sign Aquarius

Mundane issues are apt to get in the way of personal freedom, so it would be just as well to make sure that your point of view is still being heard and that you don't allow the steady pace of your regular life to obscure specific issues which may be on the rise. Romance is likely to be on the cards for some Aquarians at this point in time.

2 MONDAY
Moon Age Day 12   Moon Sign Aquarius

Your ability to communicate with others is favourably highlighted now and it is clear that you intend to speak to as many people as possible today in your efforts to get ahead generally. There are few barriers in your way when it comes to getting your message across intact and, in the main, others want to help you if they can.

3 TUESDAY
Moon Age Day 13   Moon Sign Pisces

The 'work hard and play hard' ethos of your sign is definitely on display right now. Concentrate on those matters that are really important to your future and, whenever possible, integrate your career and social life. There ought to be ample opportunity once again to make an extremely good impression on all kinds of different people.

4 WEDNESDAY
Moon Age Day 14   Moon Sign Pisces

There could be a few obstacles today, particularly at work, most of which are due to differences of opinion between yourself and others. It would be wise to address these as quickly as possible and not to allow technical problems to get out of hand either. Although you stick to your guns today, you might have a tendency to do so too much.

5 THURSDAY
Moon Age Day 15   Moon Sign Aries

A few technical matters have to be ignored today if you want to get ahead quickly. Of course, it would be madness not to pay attention to safety issues and you realise this very well. It is red tape that bothers you most of all – but the signs are that you might have discovered ways to do something about it.

6 FRIDAY
Moon Age Day 16   Moon Sign Aries

In relationships, personal issues may surface, especially if someone thinks you have wronged them in the past. It's time to lay your cards on the table, but this time with some considerable care. In practical matters it is possible to have the penny and the bun right now, but once again you will need to be canny.

7 SATURDAY
Moon Age Day 17   Moon Sign Taurus

The weekend brings a state of affairs that shows little self-control on your part. However, an ill-disciplined approach to situations that you are involved in is not going to help anything at this time. On the contrary, if you don't keep a close eye on circumstances generally, a few of them are likely to run out of control.

8 SUNDAY
Moon Age Day 18   Moon Sign Taurus

There is a strong emphasis on communication today, and specifically on coming to terms with younger people. They might think they have all the answers and so there is no point in trying to bulldoze them with your own point of view. Lead by example, show patience, and all should eventually be well.

9 MONDAY
Moon Age Day 19   Moon Sign Taurus

A few irritations appear to be more or less inevitable at the moment, and generally speaking these are likely to come from the direction of relatives or friends. Don't allow these to subvert your own plans and treat little issues to a dose of common sense. It is the wider spectrum of life that you should address right now.

10 TUESDAY   *Moon Age Day 20   Moon Sign Gemini*

Today introduces an opportunity to broaden your horizons in ways that you may not have thought of before. Grasp the nettle firmly and take the chance to push your influence with others. If you have some grandiose new scheme it is definitely time to get others on your side and you have the skills to do so.

11 WEDNESDAY   *Moon Age Day 21   Moon Sign Gemini*

Although you cannot please all of the people, all of the time, there's a good chance you get close to doing so. The fact is that you are as charming as can be right now, something that others could hardly fail to register. Some jobs will take a good deal longer than you expected but it is simply a matter of carrying on steadily.

12 THURSDAY   *Moon Age Day 22   Moon Sign Cancer*

There are some potentially lucrative ideas around now, most of which you take on board easily and instinctively. Getting others to go along with you won't be easy, particularly if you have failed to think matters through as carefully as you should have. In at least one respect you can expect a breakthrough.

13 FRIDAY   *Moon Age Day 23   Moon Sign Cancer*

Getting down to brass tacks in your conversations with other people is absolutely vital at this time. There is absolutely no point at the moment in being so diplomatic that those around you fail to understand completely what you are trying to say. Fortunately, there is a middle path that you can usually locate.

14 SATURDAY   *Moon Age Day 24   Moon Sign Leo*

Getting ahead quite as easily as you may wish isn't going to be easy with the lunar low around. Why try? This Saturday offers you the perfect opportunity to sit and watch life go by for a while. You will feel much better if you take a break and will be better equipped to make use of favourable trends later in the coming week.

15 SUNDAY
Moon Age Day 25   Moon Sign Leo

This is not necessarily a period of self-gain, it really depends on the way you approach specific situations. Go slow and steady, weighing up the pros and cons in each case. The more carefully you address details, the greater is the likelihood of success in the end.

16 MONDAY
Moon Age Day 26   Moon Sign Virgo

You may need the bright lights of the social world to cheer you up today. There are a number of astrological reasons to explain why you are slightly down in the dumps, though there is no real reason to let these spoil your day. Keep in the mainstream at work and avoid unnecessary controversy.

17 TUESDAY
Moon Age Day 27   Moon Sign Virgo

Some skilful manoeuvring may be necessary if you want to avoid family members falling out with each other. Although you won't necessarily make much material progress today, your ability to sort out the problems of those around you should be pleasing enough in its own right.

18 WEDNESDAY
Moon Age Day 28   Moon Sign Libra

This is a good day to be on the move and to be saying what you think, especially about practical situations. The real gains in today might well be romantic. New attachments should be working well under prevailing trends, whilst established ones seem to have new zest and vitality that you are bringing to them.

19 THURSDAY
Moon Age Day 29   Moon Sign Libra

The best advice that can be offered to Aquarius today is to ensure that you get one task out of the way before you start on another. There is a danger of overlap and confusion that you could so easily avoid. Trends do suggest, though, that there ought to be a good deal of happiness about in a family and friendship sense.

20 FRIDAY · *Moon Age Day 0 · Moon Sign Libra*

All joint financial matters are especially well-starred at present, likewise partnerships with a monetary aspect to them. In addition, you should find it easier to whisper those intimate little words that can make all the difference in the relationship stakes. Don't be too quick to jump to conclusions in work matters.

21 SATURDAY · *Moon Age Day 1 · Moon Sign Scorpio*

Improved communication is likely to be the best gift of the weekend. Don't be tardy when it comes to expressing an opinion, even when you know there are people around who will not agree with you. Although you won't be feeling absolutely positive about everything, you can fool others and even yourself in the end.

22 SUNDAY · *Moon Age Day 2 · Moon Sign Scorpio*

There is now a greater emphasis on professional issues, despite the fact that you probably won't even be at work right now. Planning ahead is essential and it would certainly not be advisable to leave anything until the last minute. If you feel you are running out of steam in some way, enlist a little positive support.

23 MONDAY · *Moon Age Day 3 · Moon Sign Sagittarius*

There are certain signposts to success around now, even if you have to keep your eyes wide open in order to recognise them. Socially speaking, you are anxious to meet new people and may well give some of your associations from the past the order of the boot. Aquarius is all about change and diversity at present.

24 TUESDAY · *Moon Age Day 4 · Moon Sign Sagittarius*

You could find the opinions of other to be either irrelevant or perhaps downright annoying now. It is important not to react too strongly so keep your cool. It is possible for you to score some singular successes, simply by refusing to rise to any bait that is presently offered and sticking to what you know to be right.

25 WEDNESDAY *Moon Age Day 5   Moon Sign Sagittarius*

Career matters should now be looking good. If you are in full time education, expect some good marks and compliments from tutors. Home-based activities could be slightly less than appealing, though you might have to turn your mind in that direction, if only to please your loved ones.

26 THURSDAY *Moon Age Day 6   Moon Sign Capricorn*

Your mind seems to be much more focused and the ability to see the most distant horizon in your life should be a piece of cake. Trends suggest that you can expect a little frustration arising from people who do things without checking, which could lead to a few problems for you further down the line.

27 FRIDAY *Moon Age Day 7   Moon Sign Capricorn*

Don't be dissuaded from doing things your own way. If you put yourself out too much to accommodate the ideas of others, no matter how close they may be, you could be in for a loss of some sort. When your intuition tells you to take a specific course of action, it would be sensible to heed it.

28 SATURDAY *Moon Age Day 8   Moon Sign Aquarius*

Planetary benefits come along from a number of different directions whilst the lunar high is present. You can afford to back your hunches and might find yourself sought out by someone you think of as being extremely special. Although the summer has now definitely gone you may decide to spend time out of doors.

29 SUNDAY *Moon Age Day 9   Moon Sign Aquarius*

Plans should be turning out more or less as you would expect, leaving you with hours on your hands that can be simply used for having fun. There are some particularly interesting people around, one or two of whom have had their eyes on you for a while. Affection comes from some very surprising directions.

30 MONDAY   *Moon Age Day 10   Moon Sign Pisces*

The potential for getting what you want in almost any area of life is strong today. There are people around who actively want to offer you help and support and you should be able to locate them easily enough. Conforming to the expectations that older relatives have of you could be somewhat complicated.

31 TUESDAY   *Moon Age Day 11   Moon Sign Pisces*

In debates or discussions, you are clearly up against people with strong egos at the moment. However, remember that there is more than one way to skin a cat. If you remain absolutely charming and don't rise to the bait, you will get your own way by default. Aquarius can be extremely cunning on occasions.

November 2017

1 WEDNESDAY   *Moon Age Day 12   Moon Sign Pisces*

The progressive trends you have been experiencing for a while now tend to continue, bringing you more influence and a greater degree of control over the circumstances of your own life. Friends should be especially helpful today and might even assist you in the direction of a much-cherished ambition.

2 THURSDAY   *Moon Age Day 13   Moon Sign Aries*

Communications with people in the professional world could suffer a little today, maybe because you are not quite as friendly as has been the case in the recent past. In some ways you seek to isolate yourself and could even be somewhat prickly if you feel yourself threatened or undermined in any way.

3 FRIDAY   *Moon Age Day 14   Moon Sign Aries*

This is another day on which your personal influence may be hampered in a number of different ways. Don't be afraid to allow yourself to show some vulnerability because this merely makes you look all the more human when viewed through the eyes of other people. You have a lot on your plate, so take things steadily.

4 SATURDAY   *Moon Age Day 15   Moon Sign Taurus*

Now is the time to be yourself and to make room in your life for a few small, personal indulgences. Although you are still going to be quite active, there ought to be interludes during which you can please yourself and yet manage to help others too. Diversity is important in personal interests.

5 SUNDAY
Moon Age Day 16   Moon Sign Taurus

A fast pace of events in the social world is to be expected today. There won't always be time to pick your words quite as carefully as you might wish and so it is extra important to at least try to think before you speak. The only danger here is that you will offer offence when none was intended.

6 MONDAY
Moon Age Day 17   Moon Sign Gemini

You should not have to go it alone today. It appears that there are many people who will lend a hand when you need it the most. If you do find yourself isolated, the fault could be your own. There are occasions when Aquarius shows itself to be too proud for its own good and today might be an example of this.

7 TUESDAY
Moon Age Day 18   Moon Sign Gemini

Socially speaking, this continues to be a very fulfilling period which may offer you the chance to get on-side with people who haven't played a significant role in your life up to now. Relatives and friends alike might have plans for next weekend but you might be inclined to want to keep your options open.

8 WEDNESDAY
Moon Age Day 19   Moon Sign Cancer

A socially motivated period continues, though of course that isn't at all strange for your zodiac sign, so you may not even take too much notice of it. Whispering words of love into the right ear could prove interesting today and will show your partner how you really feel during a busy period.

9 THURSDAY
Moon Age Day 20   Moon Sign Cancer

Get as much done as you can early in the day because later on there are social trends calling out to you. The weekend is already in view and you could have yourself a fine old time in the evening. Love plays a significant part in your thinking and you could be spending a significant amount of time with family members.

10 FRIDAY
Moon Age Day 21   Moon Sign Leo

The lunar low brings a planetary lull, just in time for Friday morning. The bearing this has on your life really depends on your attitude. As long as you are willing to take comfort in small things, and can shelve some of your most grandiose schemes for just a couple of days, all should be well.

11 SATURDAY
Moon Age Day 22   Moon Sign Leo

Today is a day to settle for smaller, less demanding plans. Saturday should bring feelings of peace and contentment, together with a willingness to listen to what other people are saying. If you make the most of this opportunity, you could find that the lunar low this time around has turned out to be a blessing in disguise.

12 SUNDAY
Moon Age Day 23   Moon Sign Virgo

A sense of freedom is vitally important now and you won't take kindly to being thwarted when you really feel that you need to get your own way. Travel could be uppermost in your mind and it is clear that you have a particular vision regarding the future. A degree of compromise is called for, but not too much.

13 MONDAY
Moon Age Day 24   Moon Sign Virgo

Loved ones and intimates require careful handling today. If there are sensitive issues to deal with your jokey sense of humour may not be appropriate and you may need to exercise a degree of patience, especially with people whose thought processes are not as quick as your own. Create some interesting interludes for family members.

14 TUESDAY
Moon Age Day 25   Moon Sign Libra

Although you could be rather impatient with material obligations today, you will have to get these out of the way before you can begin to move forward in certain respects. It isn't so much what people need of you that can irritate, more what some of them expect. It is very important to keep your cool.

15 WEDNESDAY   *Moon Age Day 26   Moon Sign Libra*

Being on the move can be quite rewarding. This is certainly not a
time to be standing still or to allow the grass to grow under your
feet with regard to exciting new plans. You will be amazed just how
much work you can get through right now, some of which is ably
assisted by friends.

16 THURSDAY   *Moon Age Day 27   Moon Sign Libra*

The emphasis today is on life's more playful aspects. It might be
hard to take anything particularly seriously, at least for a day or two.
However, your offbeat sense of humour and off-the-wall attitude
will be popular with almost everyone and may actually lead to you
achieving a great deal.

17 FRIDAY   *Moon Age Day 28   Moon Sign Scorpio*

Be careful when it comes to listening to gossip. There is a good
chance that much of what you hear today is either misleading or
downright wrong. Opt for some fresh air if you can. At this point
in time locking yourself inside the house won't be good for you,
mentally or physically.

18 SATURDAY   *Moon Age Day 0   Moon Sign Scorpio*

This is a particularly good time for any involvement in intellectual
interests or philosophical investigation. All Aquarians want to know
what makes the world the way it is and speculation is very healthy
for you. Of course, you won't get all the answers to the world's
problems, but you can have fun trying.

19 SUNDAY   *Moon Age Day 1   Moon Sign Sagittarius*

Though some obstacles may get in the way if you are at work, socially
and romantically, you appear to be on top form. Consideration for
family members and friends comes as second nature, though you
won't always be able to help them quite to the extent you might
wish. The generally progressive phase continues.

20 MONDAY · Moon Age Day 2 · Moon Sign Sagittarius

You could be rather socially reluctant today, which might not appear to bode well for a new week. Take comfort from the fact that this concern is probably groundless. You are likely to be very good when mixing with people you know well and your degree of reserve will be restricted to the times when you have to deal with those you don't know so well.

21 TUESDAY · Moon Age Day 3 · Moon Sign Sagittarius

This is a day to broaden your mind. There are a few complications possible but each of them teaches you something more about life and the best way to live it. Boredom is unlikely and it appears that you will find newer and better ways to show both your affection and genuine concern for others.

22 WEDNESDAY · Moon Age Day 4 · Moon Sign Capricorn

The instinct for skilful money-making is strong at the moment. There are ways and means to bring more cash into your life and you will recognise most of them. Although you could find the going a little tough in terms of casual friendships, the people who love you the most won't let you down.

23 THURSDAY · Moon Age Day 5 · Moon Sign Capricorn

It looks as though professional matters are well-starred at the moment, even if it doesn't seem to be that way at first. When you are faced with awkward people today, turn on that natural charm and watch situations change quickly. Prepare to have to show a good deal of give and take in romantic attachments.

24 FRIDAY · Moon Age Day 6 · Moon Sign Aquarius

The lunar high finds you fighting fit and anxious to make the best sort of impression. If there is any fly in the ointment at all, it could be that not everyone you come across is equally helpful. Put your best foot forward at work but leave time for personal enjoyment coming your way later in the day.

25 SATURDAY   *Moon Age Day 7   Moon Sign Aquarius*

The go-ahead influence continues and you find people rather more willing to live with your suggestions now. Part of the reason for this is your persuasive tongue and you won't have much trouble bringing people round to your point of view. Romance is especially well highlighted for those on the lookout for love.

26 SUNDAY   *Moon Age Day 8   Moon Sign Aquarius*

Your more charming and playful side is now clearly on display. Don't be too distracted by the fun and games that are available because there is plenty for you to do in practical sense. Trends suggest that many Aquarians will now be looking at the possibility of making changes to their living environments.

27 MONDAY   *Moon Age Day 9   Moon Sign Pisces*

Work and professional matters should prove more than fulfilling. Even if you don't have to toil professionally today, you will find something to keep you occupied. Physical activity is very good for you, as long as you don't do the usual Air-sign trick and overdo it. Moderation in all things is the key.

28 TUESDAY   *Moon Age Day 10   Moon Sign Pisces*

Challenges are likely, as are confrontations because now you are not likely to be willing to sit back and watch others lord it over you. On the contrary, you are not only competitive at present but also probably more than willing to defend yourself before you have even been attacked. Learn how to take a breath and count to ten before you act.

29 WEDNESDAY   *Moon Age Day 11   Moon Sign Aries*

The focus now shifts to the social arena. If there are any invitations on offer today, grab them with both hands. You need the support of friends and relatives if you are going to get the very best out of any given situation. What you definitely don't need is to be nagged, so stay away from people who insist on moaning about anything you do.

30 THURSDAY
Moon Age Day 12   Moon Sign Aries

If you find yourself under any pressure today, it is likely to come
from the direction of people who could be a little jealous of you.
Take this situation in your stride because this is definitely not a day
to give as good as you get. By remaining composed, you will win
the battle in the end.

December

2017

1 FRIDAY
Moon Age Day 13   Moon Sign Taurus

It's the first day of December and you won't want to let any opportunity pass you by at this time. From a social point of view the day should be very enjoyable as you know what you want from new encounters. Don't be slow to ask for a favour, particularly from people who are always willing to lend a hand.

2 SATURDAY
Moon Age Day 14   Moon Sign Taurus

Your go-getting side is certainly on display at present. With masses of energy, an original way of seeing things and plenty of charm, you should have little difficulty impressing some pretty important people. Although a good time socially speaking, today revolves primarily around work and practical issues.

3 SUNDAY
☿ *Moon Age Day 15   Moon Sign Gemini*

Personal indulgences would be good today but there isn't really all that much time to enjoy them. You should be able to succeed, perhaps even against some very formidable odds. In a way, the more difficult situations are the better you like them right now. Avoid routines or anything dull that holds little interest for you at present.

4 MONDAY
☿ *Moon Age Day 16   Moon Sign Gemini*

Though your love life might not be offering everything you would wish, it is possible to pep things up with just a little effort on your part. Any minor health problems should become less of a concern now, particularly since you are willing to take things easily, and perhaps even delegate some responsibilities.

5 TUESDAY ☿ *Moon Age Day 17 Moon Sign Cancer*

When it comes to matters associated with money it appears that your rather happy-go-lucky nature isn't so useful at present. Trends suggest that you need to count the pennies carefully, making certain that you are not taking financial risks or spending needlessly on luxuries you don't even really want.

6 WEDNESDAY ☿ *Moon Age Day 18 Moon Sign Cancer*

There should be a greater sense of adventure showing itself today, which is something of a pity bearing in mind that the month's lunar low begins tomorrow. For the moment, push forward progressively and embrace change. Relationships ought to be working especially well at the moment.

7 THURSDAY ☿ *Moon Age Day 19 Moon Sign Leo*

A rest period is called for, and today offers all the right circumstances to get one. Don't rush your fences and be willing to allow others to take some of the strain. You should find that you have friends who care about you deeply, as well as relatives who are quite willing to put themselves out on your account.

8 FRIDAY ☿ *Moon Age Day 20 Moon Sign Leo*

Although the lull patch is still in operation, things ought to speed up noticeably towards the middle of the day. That old friend of yours, wanderlust, begins to play a part in your thinking and you won't take kindly to be being trapped in situations you see as being distinctly boring.

9 SATURDAY ☿ *Moon Age Day 21 Moon Sign Virgo*

Encounters with new people who come into your life could prove to be something of an inspiration now. Someone, somewhere seeks to offer you some timely advice and it would be at least sensible to listen, even if you decide to follow your own path in any case. Trends move on and all in all, this should be a positive day.

10 SUNDAY   ☿   *Moon Age Day 22   Moon Sign Virgo*

Simple conversation is what proves to be most useful today. The things you hear as you move about from place to place could inspire you in some way and might lead to ideas that can mature in the fullness of time. Although you can be of tremendous use to friends, there are some things you cannot do for them.

11 MONDAY   ☿   *Moon Age Day 23   Moon Sign Virgo*

Relationships might be something of a struggle to deal with at the beginning of this working week. In games of chance or sporting activities you clearly have your wits about you and might enjoy some successful results. Don't gloat over your achievements, though. It isn't necessary and only cheapens your winning streak.

12 TUESDAY   ☿   *Moon Age Day 24   Moon Sign Libra*

An important plan could miss the target unless you make absolutely sure of all the details. It can't be stressed enough now how important it is to check and double-check. If you are careful, something you have wanted for ages could be coming your way at any time now, but if you are sloppy you may be disappointed.

13 WEDNESDAY ☿   *Moon Age Day 25   Moon Sign Libra*

Professionally speaking, the present position of the Moon brings a more stable and easy-to-read phase. Contributing to your own eventual success isn't difficult, even though you have half an eye on the festive period that lies before you. Confidence is strong when you are dealing with matters you understand.

14 THURSDAY ☿   *Moon Age Day 26   Moon Sign Scorpio*

Your social life is still on a roll and it looks as though some Aquarians will be starting Christmas very early this year. Give yourself time to take in something that is both interesting and educational and don't rush your fences where new skills are concerned. Most important of all, realise how close the holidays are.

15 FRIDAY ☿ *Moon Age Day 27 Moon Sign Scorpio*

You are best suited to working alone for the moment. This does not mean you are antisocial in any way but merely that you know what needs to be done and how to go about it. Once the responsibilities of the day are over, you should be pleased to mix freely and to be as co-operative as is necessary.

16 SATURDAY ☿ *Moon Age Day 28 Moon Sign Scorpio*

Put all thoughts of work behind you if you are an Aquarian who has the weekend to yourself. Now comes a time when you can think specifically about romance and the social side of life. This might be just about the first time that you have realised that Christmas is just around the corner and if so, make the most of the opportunities the season offers.

17 SUNDAY ☿ *Moon Age Day 29 Moon Sign Sagittarius*

Although there are plenty of people around you at the moment, this is one of those days when you are inclined to make decisions more or less independently. This does not mean locking yourself away in a darkened room for hours at a stretch, but present trends do indicate that you may not be susceptible to the influence of others.

18 MONDAY ☿ *Moon Age Day 0 Moon Sign Sagittarius*

Gradually, you find yourself identifying more with the needs and aspirations of the group and that means as the month wears on any recent solitary tendencies are inclined to disappear. The quirky side of Aquarius begins to show more, though in ways that make your relatives and friends smile.

19 TUESDAY ☿ *Moon Age Day 1 Moon Sign Capricorn*

Your general manner is somewhat blunter today than might be expected for Aquarius and you should exercise a good deal of patience when dealing with people who are naturally inclined to get on your nerves. You can easily use present trends to get ahead, though you probably also really need to lighten up somewhat.

20 WEDNESDAY ☿ *Moon Age Day 2   Moon Sign Capricorn*

This ought to be a good period for getting about socially and for finding new ways to enjoy yourself. Perhaps you are already in the middle of festive social occasions, or else pepping up the romantic side of your life. Whatever your choice, life finds ways and means to accommodate you.

21 THURSDAY ☿ *Moon Age Day 3   Moon Sign Capricorn*

This is a day on which it would be wise to follow your instincts, which are unlikely to let you down. Although not everyone you meet at present is equally reliable, it ought to be fairly easy for you to sort out the wheat from the chaff. Turn up your intuition and listen carefully to what it is telling you.

22 FRIDAY ☿ *Moon Age Day 4   Moon Sign Aquarius*

Now the lunar high is really on your side, making the run-up to Christmas perhaps the best interlude during December. Give and take in family matters is noticed and gains you some important allies. Affairs of the heart are positively highlighted and it isn't at all hard to make a good impression.

23 SATURDAY *Moon Age Day 5   Moon Sign Aquarius*

When it comes to voicing your opinions it appears that you are only too willing to have your say. Good fortune is still on your side, but you may tend to push your luck somewhat more than is good for you. Try to curb your enthusiasm just a little and don't be too quick to volunteer for anything.

24 SUNDAY *Moon Age Day 6   Moon Sign Pisces*

Christmas Eve may well set a fast pace and in fact before it is over you could be quite tired. Spread your efforts socially and don't let people monopolise you. The fact is that family and friends deserve at least some of your time, particularly younger people at this special time of the year.

25 MONDAY
Moon Age Day 7   Moon Sign Pisces

There is absolutely no doubt that your typical Aquarian nature can so easily bring out the best in others. You have plenty to keep you busy, both inside the family and further afield. This is unlikely to be a totally stay-at-home sort of Christmas Day for many Aquarians and a little excitement is quite possible.

26 TUESDAY
Moon Age Day 8   Moon Sign Pisces

Your social life generally, and your association with people you love especially, sets today apart as being quite special. There is a quiet side to your nature all the same and you might choose to spend some time watching an old movie or perhaps reading a good book. Don't be surprised if you are very nostalgic today.

27 WEDNESDAY
Moon Age Day 9   Moon Sign Aries

This is a really good time to keep your eyes and ears open. All manner of opportunities are at hand and you don't want to miss any of them. On a cautionary note, though, take what others are saying with a pinch of salt because it is entirely possible they are either joking, or trying to fool you in some way.

28 THURSDAY
Moon Age Day 10   Moon Sign Aries

For some Aquarians there is likely to be a new or renewed romantic interest to think about. Trends suggest that you should be fully committed to having a good time, particularly this evening. A few family responsibilities may crowd in during the day but you will find time later to pop a few more corks.

29 FRIDAY
Moon Age Day 11   Moon Sign Taurus

You can afford to exploit the general good luck that surrounds you at present and it is more or less certain that your organisational skills are well honed for the moment. It appears you are now better at expressing your opinions in ways that others find easier to understand and you are clearly exhibiting your sense of fun.

30 SATURDAY   *Moon Age Day 12*   *Moon Sign Taurus*

When it comes to organising your home life, you should be extremely co-operative and anxious to show just how giving you can be. This is in stark contrast to the more decisive qualities you possess. As a result, there could be a few people around who find this polarity difficult to understand and are confused by your present laid-back approach.

31 SUNDAY   *Moon Age Day 13*   *Moon Sign Gemini*

New Year's Eve finds you busier than ever and quite happy to take on any number of new responsibilities. You see the year ahead in terms of a wide road that can lead to some exciting places. So positive is your attitude at present that party time tonight is likely to be particularly special, perhaps even quite magical.

AQUARIUS:
2018 DIARY PAGES

AQUARIUS:
YOUR YEAR IN BRIEF

January and February are definitely the time for you to get going. There are so many new opportunities waiting for you and even if you are not a great lover of the winter, you will in any case have your sights set on a period later in the year. Little will hold you back and you seem to be at your most optimistic, which has to be an advantage. Routines will not suit you at all so look for plenty of variety and keep striving to find newer and better ways of getting what you want from life.

It's possible that March and April will find you in a quiet and contemplative mood. This is more of a time for consolidation and for getting to grips with issues you see as being very important to your longer-term success. Money matters should be easy to deal with and there could also be a chance for some out-of-season travel.

With the arrival of the early summer you start to come into your own in both a material and a personal sense. The attitude of loved ones can be somewhat surprising during May and June and you might have to make some changes in order to accommodate the sensibilities of those around you. This is a great time for love and a period when Aquarians who have been on their own for a while could be finding a significant other.

July and August bring some restless trends and will incline you to want to be almost anywhere that you are not. This does not mean you are likely to be unhappy. On the contrary, you might be restless but content to be that way. Take your partner or friends along on some of your adventures, all of which help to increase your confidence. Money matters should be solid and you seem to have a great way of making things work out well.

As autumn arrives you may run a little out of steam. A thoughtful mood dominates much of September and October, and it is during this period that you centre your efforts on home and family, often in a very practical way. Don't be put off by people who don't know what they are doing, even if they keep up a good pretence, but follow your own motivations and ideas.

November and December should be fairly eventful, even if from time to time it appears that you can't get exactly what you want instantaneously. Providence will look after you and so it is important to keep faith with your plans and to keep going down previously chosen paths. Christmas should be warm and happy, although perhaps a little low key, but optimism bounces back in time for the New Year.

January 2018

1 MONDAY
Moon Age Day 14   Moon Sign Gemini

As the new year begins, those you meet socially, or at work if you are there today, can prove to be very stimulating and may offer you some welcome advice. Even the most apparently insignificant information can prove to be important at present so keep your ears open. Aquarius isn't averse to a little gossip and there's plenty of that about now.

2 TUESDAY
Moon Age Day 15   Moon Sign Cancer

Whilst it might be plain that domestic partners have your best interests at heart this Tuesday the same may not be the case out there in the wider world. Avoid signing any important documents today or taking on commitments about which you are not entirely certain. A slight delay can't hurt much and will give you time to think.

3 WEDNESDAY
Moon Age Day 16   Moon Sign Cancer

You are now very busy, either out and about or at the very least inside your own head. The Aquarian mind is rarely still for long and you will be keen to follow up on ideas that began to germinate late last week. People should respond pretty much the way you expect and if they don't, you have the persuasive powers to bring them round.

4 THURSDAY
Moon Age Day 17   Moon Sign Leo

The Moon enters Leo today, which is your opposite zodiac sign. This brings a two-day period that crops up each month and which is known as the lunar low. Extra pressure seems to be surrounding you, whilst getting ahead today could seem like walking through treacle. It might be best to leave some of the real work to others.

5 FRIDAY
Moon Age Day 18   Moon Sign Leo

Don't expect everything to go exactly as you might have planned and be willing to stand back and think again if you know in your heart it is necessary to do so. There are reversals today but none of these should prove to be either serious or long lasting. Instead of trying to fight against the tide, take some time out to wallow in the shallows.

6 SATURDAY
Moon Age Day 19   Moon Sign Virgo

Although it would be very sensible to think before you act today there could be certain occasions when there simply isn't time. That's where your instincts come in and these are honed to perfection under today's trends. Few people could hope to get ahead of you in the career stakes and you shine like a star when it social settings.

7 SUNDAY
Moon Age Day 20   Moon Sign Virgo

To say that you can get noticed at present is an understatement. Aquarius can be one of the most chatty and likeable signs of the zodiac and there is certainly no doubt about that fact just now. Make the most of these positive trends by staying in good company. There is no point in hiding your true potential today.

8 MONDAY
Moon Age Day 21   Moon Sign Libra

Your ambitions are fired up and you are quite willing to step forward and be counted when it comes to new responsibilities. Not everyone is completely on your side today but a little competition does you no real harm at all and, on the contrary, leads you to hone your intellect. Don't give out standard responses today but try something new.

9 TUESDAY
Moon Age Day 22   Moon Sign Libra

There is no doubt that your ambitions are really fired up at present and you have what it takes to get what you want from life and people. That doesn't mean you can bulldoze your ideas through and it is vitally important today that you explain yourself carefully and also listen to points of view that might be very different than yours.

10 WEDNESDAY · · · · · · *Moon Age Day 23 · · · Moon Sign Scorpio*

Though optimism and positive thinking are important at the present time you also need to be resting on occasion and allowing some situations to sort themselves out. Routines can be fairly comfortable for now and it would be very easy to settle back and allow colleagues to take most of the strain – but it won't happen, will it?

11 THURSDAY · · · · · · *Moon Age Day 24 · · · Moon Sign Scorpio*

When it comes to making agreements with others, take care at the moment not to get yourself involved in situations from which it would be better to be disassociated. Look out for gifts coming your way later in the day – even if these are not wrapped in paper and tied with ribbons they should be very welcome.

12 FRIDAY · · · · · · *Moon Age Day 25 · · · Moon Sign Scorpio*

Avoid arguing over details today because it is the broader spectrum of life that matters the most. If you go with the flow instead of trying to tinker with things you should find that happiness and success follow. A positive response to a particular suggestion made by your partner or a close family member should make everyone happy.

13 SATURDAY · · · · · · *Moon Age Day 26 · · · Moon Sign Sagittarius*

Working with people you like can be extremely satisfying today and you won't be all that keen to push yourself harder than proves to be necessary. The weather outside may not be the best, but a little fresh air and a change of scenery would do you the world of good. All work and no play can make Aquarius dull and listless.

14 SUNDAY · · · · · · *Moon Age Day 27 · · · Moon Sign Sagittarius*

The demands coming in from all directions will certainly keep you on your toes just now but you can still find a few moments for the more intimate aspects of your life. Some Aquarians will now begin to feel the need to make significant changes in or around the home but there may be very little time to act upon such desires today.

15 MONDAY *Moon Age Day 28   Moon Sign Capricorn*

You remain generally easy-going and very much in tune with your financial goals today. This is a good time for beginning new investments or changing a few existing ones and your whole attitude is incredibly expansive and outgoing. You demonstrate a good mix between the need for financial security and the desire to spread your wings.

16 TUESDAY *Moon Age Day 0   Moon Sign Capricorn*

If there are intimate issues that you know need dealing with as soon as possible, talk about them today and also listen closely to what your partner has to say. From a business point of view this time is hardly likely to prove a rip-roaring success and a little extra patience is required when you have to deal with intransigent types.

17 WEDNESDAY *Moon Age Day 1   Moon Sign Capricorn*

Activities at work should now be more enjoyable and slowly but surely you are gaining speed in your life generally. However, take heed of this word of caution: until the Sun moves away from your solar twelfth house in a few days you will still have to be careful about your financial resources so hold back from major spending just now.

18 THURSDAY *Moon Age Day 2   Moon Sign Aquarius*

Today the Moon moves into the zodiac sign of Aquarius, bringing that part of the month that is known as the lunar high. Your level of general good luck is much higher than usual and you can afford to back your hunches to a greater extent. It's true that there are changes in the offing but nearly all of these are potentially advantageous.

19 FRIDAY *Moon Age Day 3   Moon Sign Aquarius*

This is one of the best days of the month for putting new plans into operation. Don't hold back when you know in your heart that your ideas are sound and enlist the support of people who are usually only too willing to follow your lead. Not only can you do yourself good now but you can help your colleagues and friends too.

20 SATURDAY
Moon Age Day 4   Moon Sign Pisces

The accent is now upon social activities and your natural attractiveness to others. You won't have any difficulty at all bringing people round to your way of thinking and neither are you likely to be short of admirers at this time. There is a great deal of potential information coming your way, and all you have to do is sort it out.

21 SUNDAY
Moon Age Day 5   Moon Sign Pisces

Although in some ways you will be happy to settle for a distinctly quiet social scene, in other situations you will be content to be the centre of attention today. It's really a case of not knowing what you want for the moment, though times will change significantly in only a few more days. Keep a sense of proportion at work and strike a balance in all things.

22 MONDAY
Moon Age Day 6   Moon Sign Pisces

Information you may well put to good use could arrive by way of a friend, a colleague or even your partner. This is an excellent period for learning and it looks as though you can discover something that will be of great use to you in the weeks and months ahead. The time is definitely right to keep your eyes open for all sources of information.

23 TUESDAY
Moon Age Day 7   Moon Sign Aries

Professional developments are significant at this stage of the week because it is only a couple of days before great changes will become possible. Taking the odd chance right now could lead to much more than you expect and it looks as though the real Aquarius will soon be on display. For today you should plan but hold off taking action.

24 WEDNESDAY
Moon Age Day 8   Moon Sign Aries

Expect a generally positive time in your social life because trends suggest that good things should be coming your way, particularly as a result of the actions of friends and associates. It is towards your regular social group that you are most likely to turn your attention now but there could also be the odd newcomer enlivening your life.

25 THURSDAY
Moon Age Day 9   Moon Sign Taurus

Don't be moved by peculiar moods to do things that are actually very untypical for you. At the same time there may be plenty of people who think they know better than you do how your life ought to be lived. Although you won't want to be rude to anyone it's up to you now to make it plain that you know best what is right for your life.

26 FRIDAY
Moon Age Day 10   Moon Sign Taurus

The focus for the moment is on luxury and your need to feel more than comfortable with your lot in life generally. Don't overlook any new financial possibilities and keep your eyes open for bargains that are likely to come your way. There may be a few unforced errors to deal with but you are going to be positive in most of your dealings.

27 SATURDAY
Moon Age Day 11   Moon Sign Gemini

Look out for a time of self-discovery and the chance to better yourself in a number of different ways. There are many alternative ways in which to present yourself and it looks as though you will be trying them all at this juncture. Pep up your social life by doing something completely different and by making interesting new friends.

28 SUNDAY
Moon Age Day 12   Moon Sign Gemini

There is a tendency for a little self-indulgence today, so be just a little careful that you don't overdo things. Avoid eating or drinking too much and be especially cautious about alcohol at this time. As far as money is concerned you could be inclined to spoil yourself somewhat but a little time spent seeking out bargains could be time well spent.

29 MONDAY
Moon Age Day 13   Moon Sign Cancer

You are likely to be a really impressive creature in a social sense today. You will enjoy stimulating company and have everything it takes to surprise people and to put them in awe of your abilities. Most Aquarians will be laying on the charisma with a trowel today and almost everything you do will be theatrical and intended to wow others.

30 TUESDAY
Moon Age Day 14   Moon Sign Cancer

Your ambitions are driving you forward but you won't always know for sure what the destination is going to be. As a rule this is no problem to you – after all you are a child of Aquarius. Unfortunately for the moment there are going to be ifs and buts that don't normally occur. Still, there is no harm in showing a little caution now and again.

31 WEDNESDAY
Moon Age Day 15   Moon Sign Leo

You will have very little patience with jobs that bore you today and will want to free yourself from any restrictions that seem to be holding you back. Some of these may be necessary for the moment and a little extra care may be required before you put too much effort into breaking free when you don't know what you want afterwards.

February 2018

1 THURSDAY
Moon Age Day 16   Moon Sign Leo

With the Moon now in the zodiac sign of Leo you will be more reserved, less inclined to speak your mind and probably not half as sure of yourself as usual. Others, sensing that something is amiss, may think you are sulking or being unnecessarily grumpy, so it's important to at least appear cheerful, even if you have something serious on your mind.

2 FRIDAY
Moon Age Day 17   Moon Sign Virgo

Although you can expect a few tensions in personal relationships, in the main you are getting on well with almost everyone. It's true that you do have a slight air of mystery around you at the moment but that probably turns out to be a distinct advantage. There are gains to be made from keeping some people guessing.

3 SATURDAY
Moon Age Day 18   Moon Sign Virgo

Domestic and family matters may be demanding most of your attention today but there should still be moments during which you can do whatever takes your fancy. You might be in the market for a spot of shopping, and if so you can be fairly sure of getting a bargain or two. Spend some quality time later with your partner.

4 SUNDAY
Moon Age Day 19   Moon Sign Libra

Today is favourable for all business transactions and for professional partnerships. As is often the case for Aquarius you have that certain knack for mixing business with pleasure and you are likely to be meeting some very interesting individuals around this time. Confronting an issue from the past is also likely sometime today.

5 MONDAY
Moon Age Day 20   Moon Sign Libra

Diversity is now the key to real happiness – not that this is very unusual for you. What would bore you today would be to get stuck in a rut and to have little chance of making the progress in life that you sense is possible around now. For this reason you should avoid mixing with people who move at the pace of a tortoise.

6 TUESDAY
Moon Age Day 21   Moon Sign Libra

Today you will get on extremely well with people who have a happy-go-lucky attitude and who are willing to bend with the wind. Once again you find difficulties if you allow yourself to be surrounded by pessimists. Your own attitude to life at the moment is a little like throwing stones in ponds to see how big the splashes are.

7 WEDNESDAY
Moon Age Day 22   Moon Sign Scorpio

A little restructuring of your personal life may seem to be necessary at the moment but move forward carefully and don't upset others by speaking too rashly or out of turn. Older family members probably have the right words of wisdom to keep you on course and it would be well worthwhile listening to what they have to say.

8 THURSDAY
Moon Age Day 23   Moon Sign Scorpio

As today wears on you should gradually find your feet more and be happier to be out there in the social mainstream. Be careful about money and check all details before getting yourself involved in some long-term project that could bring financial complications. It would be better to keep everything as simple as possible now.

9 FRIDAY
Moon Age Day 24   Moon Sign Sagittarius

Be careful today because you might just be a little too assertive for your own good. It's great to be confident and to show other people that you are so but you could be taking the wind out of someone's sails without realising it. Be especially considerate of the feelings of family members and perhaps one or two good friends.

10 SATURDAY   *Moon Age Day 25   Moon Sign Sagittarius*

Personal matters are more rewarding today than professional or practical ones. Maybe you have decided to spend more time with your partner, while unattached Aquarians should be casting around at the moment because new relationships are part of the astrological agenda. Not everyone loves you today but the most important people do.

11 SUNDAY   *Moon Age Day 26   Moon Sign Sagittarius*

It might seem warm and comfortable in your own little world today but that's not where things are likely to happen. There's just a chance you are withdrawing because there is something to be done that you don't relish. If this is the case get it out of the way as early in the day as you can, leaving you free to do more enjoyable things.

12 MONDAY   *Moon Age Day 27   Moon Sign Capricorn*

Personal issues remain at the forefront of your mind and might cause you to be more introspective than has been the case so far this year. You are hardly likely to present yourself as bold or adventurous today but you can put on a little pretence when you know there is a degree of expectation coming from the direction of others.

13 TUESDAY   *Moon Age Day 28   Moon Sign Capricorn*

You can look at matters today in a very different way and will certainly be happiest when you are left to your own devices to sort things out. The only slight fly in the ointment at the moment comes when you sense interference taking place. If there is one thing you absolutely insist on at the moment it is a certain degree of privacy.

14 WEDNESDAY   *Moon Age Day 29   Moon Sign Aquarius*

Keep up your diversity of interests and don't be so centred on one task that you fail to see how well other things are turning out. It's early in the year yet but you may decide that this would still be a good time to take a trip. Winter doesn't really bother you at all because of the time of year you were born, so get out there and have fun.

15 THURSDAY   *Moon Age Day 0*   *Moon Sign Aquarius*

What really counts at the moment is variety which, as they say, is the spice of life. That's certainly true for you and together with your unconventional way of doing things you should be attracting a good deal of attention from colleagues and friends at the moment. Help to drag a slightly reluctant family member out of a rut.

16 FRIDAY   *Moon Age Day 1*   *Moon Sign Aquarius*

You should define and then follow your own path as much as possible at this time. There is now a real chance for growth in your life and rather less confusion around you than seems to have been the case during January. Keep abreast of current news and views, especially at work, and let others know that you are around.

17 SATURDAY   *Moon Age Day 2*   *Moon Sign Pisces*

Romance and pleasure receive something of a boost today and you should be feeling quite good about the way things are going in a financial sense, too. It is possible that money will be coming from less than expected directions – even though the minute it arrives there could be bills coming in that will take some of it away again.

18 SUNDAY   *Moon Age Day 3*   *Moon Sign Pisces*

This is a time of extreme dynamism and an overriding sense of purpose. Not everyone around you seems to understand what you want or where you need to be and there are occasions when you will have to go it alone. This is probably the best time of the month to start ambitious new projects and to let the world know who you are.

19 MONDAY   *Moon Age Day 4*   *Moon Sign Aries*

It goes without saying under present trends that you have to leave certain things where they belong, firmly in the past. It's time to move on and also a good period for dumping things that are no longer of any use to you. There should be warm moments as far as your love life is concerned and a new understanding with your partner.

20 TUESDAY   *Moon Age Day 5   Moon Sign Aries*

It is possible that for today you will prefer the world of imagination and will be less than inclined to get involved in things that look as though they could be difficult. It isn't that you are retreating from the world in a general sense because you will be quite happy to socialise and to chat to colleagues. You just don't want to push hard.

21 WEDNESDAY   *Moon Age Day 6   Moon Sign Taurus*

It probably pays to look at new issues and to promote yourself more now. How can people know what you are worth when they don't even know you exist? It isn't like Aquarius to stand in the shadows and everything around you suggests that the time is right to move out into the light. Being talked about is a positive thing right now.

22 THURSDAY   *Moon Age Day 7   Moon Sign Taurus*

There is a dynamic self-confidence about today and your powers of attraction are going through the roof. This isn't simply a romantic response but can work on almost any level of your life. People generally like you but as the days pass you will discover just how popular it is possible for you to be. Keep plugging away at work.

23 FRIDAY   *Moon Age Day 8   Moon Sign Taurus*

You won't be tardy when it comes to voicing your opinions or when you need to show how positive you are capable of being. The fact is that people recognise your talents instinctively and they should be more than willing to give you a chance. Routines are for the birds today and should be left for other people to follow.

24 SATURDAY   *Moon Age Day 9   Moon Sign Gemini*

Aside from efforts you are clearly making at the moment to realise certain economic goals you are also concerned with steps you can take to improve your all-round sense of security. Almost anything can be achieved whilst you are in your present state of mind but do put some time aside to show those closest to you how you really feel.

25 SUNDAY   *Moon Age Day 10   Moon Sign Gemini*

You are extremely well disposed to people who come new into your life around this time. There could be some new friendships to be made, one or two of which might last a lifetime. With everything to play for at work it looks as though you will be celebrating Sunday with a flourish. Romantic possibilities also look good.

26 MONDAY   *Moon Age Day 11   Moon Sign Cancer*

Getting the finer things in life is part of what Aquarius is about. You love a little luxury and to be able to buy the very best sometimes. This being the case, you need to get your skates on and to be out there hustling. There are some bargains to be had but those on the selling end will fully expect you to haggle. Don't disappoint them.

27 TUESDAY   *Moon Age Day 12   Moon Sign Cancer*

Share some time with your loved ones today, even though you might find you are quite busy in a practical sense. There are ways and means of mixing business with pleasure and there is a real desire on your part to break down the barriers of doubt and potential worry. In other words you should be feeling on top form.

28 WEDNESDAY   *Moon Age Day 13   Moon Sign Leo*

You are now introspective and relish your own company more than that of other people. From your point of view this is just fine but the same people who you urged onward and upward a few days ago are now waiting for you to catch up. That comes in a day or two but for the moment you are happy to bide your time and saunter along.

March 2018

1 THURSDAY
Moon Age Day 14   Moon Sign Leo

Leave any potentially serious problems alone for the moment because you are not in the right frame of mind to deal with them. Who knows, by the time you get back to them they could have disappeared of their own accord. It may be somewhat hard to think constructively for the moment and that is a legacy of the lunar low you are under just at present.

2 FRIDAY
Moon Age Day 15   Moon Sign Virgo

You always function well in roles that require courage and the ability to confront others if it proves to be necessary. You know how to handle stress at work and you are especially capable at the moment. Any small disagreements are unlikely to bother you at all because you are too busy focusing on your chosen objectives.

3 SATURDAY
Moon Age Day 16   Moon Sign Virgo

A good time to make favourable business commitments comes along, though you may be quite worried about money for some reason. Sit down and work things out properly because it is possible you have made some sort of mistake or miscalculation. The planets are now generally on your side and they prove to be very supportive.

4 SUNDAY
Moon Age Day 17   Moon Sign Libra

You can expect a little boost to your finances now and probably also more in the way of recognition for those you care about. In a general sense it looks as though you are attracting the attention of certain people and they are likely to do you little favours you didn't expect. Leave time aside to be with family members, especially younger people.

5 MONDAY
Moon Age Day 18   Moon Sign Libra

Anything can happen at the start of this week and you really do need to keep your eye on the ball if you want to get the very most out of the day. People are busy all around you and they won't have time to stop and talk too much. That won't bother you a great deal because you want to be up there sparring with the best of them today.

6 TUESDAY
Moon Age Day 19   Moon Sign Scorpio

You are now capable of taking some tough decisions, not just for yourself but on account of other people too. If it's a case of more of the same today you could become quite bored and so a change in routines is definitely called for. You are basically a fighter right now and want to cut through to the core of issues.

7 WEDNESDAY
Moon Age Day 20   Moon Sign Scorpio

At this time business opportunities are likely to occupy at least part of your thinking. The Sun is now in your solar second house so you approach life in a practical way and will be anxious to see things being done in the way you think they should be undertaken. This makes you very good when it comes to handing out instructions.

8 THURSDAY
Moon Age Day 21   Moon Sign Sagittarius

There could be some impatience when it comes to personal restrictions, especially if you feel that you are being held back without any real justification. You are certainly anxious to get ahead but could be inclined to make complications for yourself on the way. If some people seem to be playing strange games, don't get involved.

9 FRIDAY
Moon Age Day 22   Moon Sign Sagittarius

Throw yourself into things today, even if it means spending a little money. Business opportunities are likely to come your way, some of them from fairly unexpected directions. Conforming to the expectations of other people won't always be too easy and it looks as though the unique side of your nature is now fully on display.

10 SATURDAY   *Moon Age Day 23   Moon Sign Sagittarius*

Money matters are to the fore again, as they have been for a week or two now. It may seem as if you have been working long and hard to achieve your objectives and to get your reward but things will really start to come together around now. Your partner could be demanding more of your time but that is unlikely to worry you.

11 SUNDAY   *Moon Age Day 24   Moon Sign Capricorn*

Although you need to be quite careful who you listen to today there are people around who know exactly how to point you in the right direction. The problem lies in knowing when the information is reliable. Turn up your intuition to full and, if necessary, take a leap in the dark. Your hunches are likely to be mostly correct at this time.

12 MONDAY   *Moon Age Day 25   Moon Sign Capricorn*

It may be time to look at the state of your finances again but this time with a great deal more optimism and less of a tendency to worry than was evident last week. Now you see your way forward clearly in a number of different ways and you have what it takes to convince others that your plans are sound. People want to listen to you.

13 TUESDAY   *Moon Age Day 26   Moon Sign Aquarius*

Breakthroughs in your career could open up entirely new vistas for you and should see you feeling much more contented with your lot than has been the case for the last couple of weeks at least. If there are big decisions to be made you could hardly choose a better time for making them than that presented by present planetary trends.

14 WEDNESDAY   *Moon Age Day 27   Moon Sign Aquarius*

Your thinking, talking and general powers of instinctive understanding should be good and this is a time when you can afford to take some far-reaching decisions. You are much less likely to be held back by details and would be quite happy to go with the flow regarding issues that worried you a lot before. Spend time with your family.

15 THURSDAY
Moon Age Day 28   Moon Sign Aquarius

Catch up on news and views today and keep on talking. Today is likely to prove inspirational for you and there should be opportunities to break routines and to do things that are simply interesting for their own sake. Everything you learn comes in handy at some stage, which is something Aquarius tends to realise instinctively.

16 FRIDAY
Moon Age Day 29   Moon Sign Pisces

There isn't much wrong with your cognitive powers at present and working out how to get on well should be quite easy. It is only when it comes to personal attachments that you might be somewhat blind to situations. Your confidence tells you that you are doing the right thing, but you might have to search inside yourself to be absolutely sure.

17 SATURDAY
Moon Age Day 0   Moon Sign Pisces

Opportunities for progress are around every corner, even if it might seem as though you need a periscope to see them. Fortunately you have great insight into the behaviour of others and a good deal of intuition at the moment. Take these, add a little common sense and it seems as though you have the best recipe for success.

18 SUNDAY
Moon Age Day 1   Moon Sign Aries

You might expect to be at the forefront of things from a social perspective but there are jobs that need to be done first. This can turn out to be rather frustrating because you seem to jog along from one rather tedious task to another. Nevertheless if you persevere you should find part of the day that you can truly call your own.

19 MONDAY
Moon Age Day 2   Moon Sign Aries

This is a time for togetherness in at least one sense. You are more likely now to be drawn to home and family and will be quite happy to spend some time doing domestic things, rather than trying to push ahead all the time in the outside world. Someone you don't see very often could well come back into your life around now.

20 TUESDAY
Moon Age Day 3   Moon Sign Aries

If there is something you really want to get done – do it today. Your organisational skills are especially good and you will recognise instinctively when it is the best time to act. There are moments right now when some of the details of life pass you by but present planetary trends make it possible for you to find useful short cuts to your objectives.

21 WEDNESDAY
Moon Age Day 4   Moon Sign Taurus

Partnerships of almost any sort should be working out well for you now and this would be particularly true in the case of business associations. Although in some ways today might not seem to be the best time for making professional decisions the trends are so good that you might make an exception. Meanwhile family members amuse you.

22 THURSDAY
Moon Age Day 5   Moon Sign Taurus

You could do a lot worse today than getting together with someone you love in congenial surroundings and enjoying yourself whilst others are toiling away. If this isn't possible all through today you might have to make do with the evening instead. Make sure you get some fresh air at this time, even if it's only for a few minutes.

23 FRIDAY
☿   *Moon Age Day 6   Moon Sign Gemini*

The things that others do on your behalf are what make you feel rather special at the moment and so this ought to be a fairly smooth-running and enjoyable period for nearly all Aquarians. If there are any difficulties at present these are likely to come from the direction of your family and are as a result of your tendency to worry too much.

24 SATURDAY
☿   *Moon Age Day 7   Moon Sign Gemini*

Make good use of your very astute mind today and learn that not everything comes to you as a result of effort but sometimes thanks to pure good luck. If you fail to realise this fact something of potentially great importance could pass you by and that would be a great pity. Don't get involved in family rows but as usual sort them out.

25 SUNDAY ☿ *Moon Age Day 8   Moon Sign Cancer*

Not everything goes strictly the way you would wish but that doesn't matter at all if you keep an open mind and show yourself able to ride with the ups and downs as if you were on a roller coaster. People you love may be depending on you later in the day and you need to think rather carefully before offering them some timely advice.

26 MONDAY ☿ *Moon Age Day 9   Moon Sign Cancer*

Look towards a very harmonious period in personal matters and also recognise just how much a new friendship is adding to your life. New personalities are on the horizon all the time and they bring with them different ways of looking at existing situations. This is a day during which you need to spend time deciding what you really need for yourself.

27 TUESDAY ☿ *Moon Age Day 10   Moon Sign Leo*

Leave alone any serious intention to get on with anything quickly because today probably won't work out at all like that. You need to be steady in your approach to life and to check all details carefully. In a couple of days all should be back to normal but if you try to rush ahead right now you are likely to be in for some disappointments.

28 WEDNESDAY ☿ *Moon Age Day 11   Moon Sign Leo*

You can expect life to be slowing down a little now, and with the Moon still in Leo you should be rather circumspect about what you take on today. Spring is on the way and the weather should be improving just a little. What not get out of doors and enjoy the lengthening days? On the way you could meet the odd entertaining individual.

29 THURSDAY ☿ *Moon Age Day 12   Moon Sign Virgo*

News that comes to you via colleagues or friends could be of great importance so it is really sensible to keep your ears open today. In the main you won't miss a trick and show yourself to be alert and very reactive. You may also be just a little touchy on occasions so make sure that you count to ten before losing your temper.

30 FRIDAY ☿ *Moon Age Day 13 Moon Sign Virgo*

Aquarius is very romantically inclined at the moment and this shows itself in a number of different ways. Everyone appreciates your naturally warm nature and today you are also demonstrating just how zany and excitable you can be. There are moments right now when you could get away with saying almost anything.

31 SATURDAY ☿ *Moon Age Day 14 Moon Sign Libra*

There is plenty of concentration available to you today and if there is one particular job that has been demanding your attention for some time now, today is right for getting it sorted altogether. Aquarius is also very intuitive under present planetary trends and you can be sure that your feelings regarding someone else are quite accurate.

April

2018

1 SUNDAY ☿ *Moon Age Day 15 Moon Sign Libra*

Working your way towards a greater sense of financial security is likely to be uppermost in your mind at the moment. This is also a time when you will spend a little to make more later. Whether or not you can get family members to be more careful with cash is in some doubt, which could turn out to be slightly frustrating.

2 MONDAY ☿ *Moon Age Day 16 Moon Sign Scorpio*

Of great note around now is your ability to experiment and to come up with new ideas, particularly where your work life is concerned. A few unforced errors are also possible but in the main when these come along you will simply shrug your shoulders and try again. What really shines out now is your originality and that gets you noticed.

3 TUESDAY ☿ *Moon Age Day 17 Moon Sign Scorpio*

You now tend to be fairly optimistic and self-assured on those occasions when it matters the most. Today should give you the chance to think things through without being bothered too much by silly details. However, you will also feel fairly restless and will need to move around a good deal in one way or another.

4 WEDNESDAY ☿ *Moon Age Day 18 Moon Sign Scorpio*

Social matters are likely to look fairly vibrant around now and there will be every opportunity to get yourself better known in specific circles. The impression is that wherever you were on the back row of life you are now likely to be brought to the front. That won't bother you in the slightest because you just love to be on display.

93

5 THURSDAY   ☿ *Moon Age Day 19*   *Moon Sign Sagittarius*

There could be some good ideas on the financial front but you really do need to take a measured and thorough approach to life generally. Although this is unlikely to be the most exciting or inspirational day you will experience this month there are advantages. Many of these come about as the result of the attitude of others.

6 FRIDAY   ☿ *Moon Age Day 20*   *Moon Sign Sagittarius*

Don't expect too much peace and quiet at home. The fact is that everyone wants to talk at once and they all want to talk exclusively to you. This will hardly make for the most relaxing atmosphere but you enjoy the cut and thrust of family life and need to be needed. You might complain about the racket but it won't really bother you.

7 SATURDAY   ☿ *Moon Age Day 21*   *Moon Sign Capricorn*

You are now expressive and able to communicate well across the board. Of course there is nothing new about this for Aquarius but you might be even chattier than usual. With many different interests on offer it won't be hard to fill your Saturday and by the time the evening arrives you will be socially motivated and full of beans.

8 SUNDAY   ☿ *Moon Age Day 22*   *Moon Sign Capricorn*

This would be an ideal time for forward planning and for getting to grips with something that may have been a mystery to you in the past. In most situations you will be patient and determined and will do all you can to consolidate your position. Aquarius is extremely shrewd at the moment and nobody is likely to fool you.

9 MONDAY   ☿ *Moon Age Day 23*   *Moon Sign Capricorn*

The start of a new week shows you making every effort to split your time between work and the necessary demands that surround you at home. You feel these more keenly because of the present position of the Sun but there are other people who can do things too and you need to encourage everyone to pull their weight this week.

10 TUESDAY ☿ *Moon Age Day 24   Moon Sign Aquarius*

This is going to be a time of great excitement and very interesting possibilities. You won't get the full force of the lunar high if you stick around your house all day and there is no doubt that the best opportunities arise when you are out and about. Personal ambitions count for a great deal and friends will help you realise some of these.

11 WEDNESDAY ☿ *Moon Age Day 25   Moon Sign Aquarius*

There should be more than an element of luck to support you while the lunar high is present and you need to take advantage of situations that go your way. Following up on things is vitally important, so no laziness is allowed at the moment. New career openings are possible for some, whilst all Aquarians should be content at home.

12 THURSDAY ☿   *Moon Age Day 26   Moon Sign Pisces*

The way you influence the world at this time is by being ready to alter your attitude and your actions at a moment's notice. It is the very adaptability of Aquarius that proves to be its best ally and this is certainly going to be the case right now. Today could be extremely inspiring in all sorts of ways so get out and about in as many different areas as you can.

13 FRIDAY ☿   *Moon Age Day 27   Moon Sign Pisces*

You will be extremely mentally active during most of today and should really be seeking out new challenges that tax your intellect and which keep you busy. There should not be anything particularly difficult about the practical side of life but you might have to be extra diplomatic in your dealings with your partner.

14 SATURDAY ☿   *Moon Age Day 28   Moon Sign Pisces*

Issues of economic security could seem urgent and you will feel a strong drive to overcome what you see as being any weakness in this area of your life. Avoid too much self-indulgence today and be especially careful about what you are eating. Too much of a good thing is definitely not an advantage to the average Aquarian.

15 SUNDAY   *Moon Age Day 29   Moon Sign Aries*

If you are romantically involved you should experience some definite high points today. As part of a couple things go better around this time and if you have yet to commit yourself to a particular relationship it is more than possible that you will be doing so now. Get onside with winners at work and do your very best.

16 MONDAY   *Moon Age Day 0   Moon Sign Aries*

You are likely to have rather a busy schedule now and with Mars in its present position you will also want to organise things very carefully indeed. You can score instant successes and will be extremely competitive when at work. Don't dedicate yourself wholly to making money because there are also good social trends around.

17 TUESDAY   *Moon Age Day 1   Moon Sign Taurus*

You will benefit now from a lifestyle that brings you into closer proximity to people who were strangers just a short while ago. Your natural tendency to co-operate is significantly heightened at this time and there are instances when getting onside with colleagues can be especially helpful. Don't pass up opportunities to shine socially.

18 WEDNESDAY   *Moon Age Day 2   Moon Sign Taurus*

Existing relationships receive a definite boost, though for some Aquarians it is likely to be a case of 'all change'. Whatever you decide to do it is important to move forward with confidence and as if you know what you are doing. Even on the occasions when you do not, it looks as though you will have enough cheek to fool almost anyone.

19 THURSDAY   *Moon Age Day 3   Moon Sign Gemini*

Your ability to take the starring role in a social sense can be put to great practical use at the moment. It will also be quite easy to mix business with pleasure in some way. Recent plans are likely to come under the spotlight and it will not simply be you who wants to look at and discuss them. Commonality is the key when you are with others.

20 FRIDAY *Moon Age Day 4   Moon Sign Gemini*

This would be an excellent time during which to attend to all those little details that others have forgotten about. If there is any resentment about at all today it could be that you feel slightly annoyed that you have to sort out jobs that are not strictly your own. However, by the time you can complain everything could be sorted out.

21 SATURDAY *Moon Age Day 5   Moon Sign Cancer*

Domestic and family issues demand a good deal of your attention for the next few weeks and this is because the Sun has now moved in to your solar fourth house. Of course you won't be tied up with such thoughts all the time but there isn't much doubt that you are likely to be more concerned than usual for those with whom you live.

22 SUNDAY *Moon Age Day 6   Moon Sign Cancer*

You may have to get rid of something – perhaps permanently, because that is part of the meaning of the Sun in its present position. Nobody will be pushing you into doing anything that goes against the grain but it will be a natural impulse across the next three or four weeks to shed those things you don't need and to move forward.

23 MONDAY *Moon Age Day 7   Moon Sign Leo*

The lunar low is around during today and this can take the wind out of your sails in some respects. From a social point of view you will remain on top form but you probably won't have your usual amount of energy and will gain from short periods of rest. Keep stimulating your mind because you need to feel challenged.

24 TUESDAY *Moon Age Day 8   Moon Sign Leo*

This ought to be a good day for thinking but not an especially fortunate time for doing too much. There is a good chance that if you take on anything too complicated you will have to do it again because you are not as dextrous as would usually be the case. Concentrate on personal attachments and enjoy giving and receiving compliments.

25 WEDNESDAY   *Moon Age Day 9   Moon Sign Virgo*

Apart from good trends in shared resources this should also be a fortunate time when it comes to a renewal of your personal life and a new determination to get certain tasks out of the way once and for all. Emotional relationships should also come under the spotlight of your attention and you will be doing all you can for your partner.

26 THURSDAY   *Moon Age Day 10   Moon Sign Virgo*

You should now keep personal comments out of diplomatic discussions. You know how you feel about certain matters but that doesn't mean you have to express your opinions on every occasion. There are times when you know that an even and objective approach would work best and for the moment you need to stick to being subtle.

27 FRIDAY   *Moon Age Day 11   Moon Sign Virgo*

This could be a good time for joint commitments and for dealing with family resources after consulting others who are involved. People are naturally inclined to follow your lead at the moment, not because you are in any way forceful but rather on account of your ability to make things so clear that there can be no misunderstanding.

28 SATURDAY   *Moon Age Day 12   Moon Sign Libra*

It is in helping others that you get the most out of life under present planetary trends. Although it may not be your intention to make your own future more secure, the very fact that you are so caring is not lost on anyone. As a result you are storing up favours for later and what is more you make a good impression even when you don't realise it.

29 SUNDAY   *Moon Age Day 13   Moon Sign Libra*

There is clearly less pressure about now and you will have more time during which you can do whatever takes your fancy. The year is advancing and you will want to make the very best of each passing season. For now you could do worse than to go out with someone you love and look at the way nature is waking up all around you.

30 MONDAY
Moon Age Day 14   Moon Sign Scorpio

The issue now arises as to whether you want to continue with something as it is or institute significant changes. It all depends on how energetic you feel. On the one hand there are planetary influences pushing you forward but on the other there are trends that suggest you might be feeling somewhat lazy. The decision is yours.

May

2018

1 TUESDAY
Moon Age Day 15   Moon Sign Scorpio

You will now be at your best when you are amongst close friends or at the very least with people you know are fond of you. Don't be in the least surprised if you discover you have an admirer you didn't know about because you come across as being very attractive at the moment. This should be a good week to shine romantically.

2 WEDNESDAY
Moon Age Day 16   Moon Sign Sagittarius

Avoid getting into unnecessary and pointless discussions with others. There is nothing wrong with disagreeing but this could so easily turn into arguments now and you haven't got the time to be at odds with people. Help others to do things in a practical sense, especially when they are trying to do something you are very good at.

3 THURSDAY
Moon Age Day 17   Moon Sign Sagittarius

There isn't much doubt about your ability to charm people under present planetary trends. Aquarius is warm and sociable at the best of times but now you turn the charisma up to full and can gain even more admirers as a result. You might not mean to make someone feel you are flirting with them, but that could be the way it seems to them.

4 FRIDAY
Moon Age Day 18   Moon Sign Sagittarius

When you are taking on new situations you must take particular care to be diplomatic with others. You know what you are doing but those around you may not, which is why you have to show as much patience as you can muster. Extremely sensitive types could be somewhat put off by any up-front style, so tact and diplomacy go a long way.

5 SATURDAY   *Moon Age Day 19   Moon Sign Capricorn*

You could find yourself at odds with others over situations that normally wouldn't be a problem to you at all. It isn't that you need to have your own way – more that those around you are being obstructive. Ignore these trends because you can be busy in other ways and won't have too much time to pick over the bones or irrelevancies.

6 SUNDAY   *Moon Age Day 20   Moon Sign Capricorn*

Romance should now be your forte and your mind goes back to a past love or to the way you once viewed a much lower-key relationship that is still present. Maybe you will be trying to recapture the past but for Aquarius that just isn't possible. It is far better to commit yourself to whatever is happening around you right now.

7 MONDAY   *Moon Age Day 21   Moon Sign Aquarius*

Like pushing a button the confusion disappears and you emerge into the bright sunshine of potential success. The lunar high comes along just as the week gets going and it offers you new starts and fresh vistas. You should feel very good about yourself today and tomorrow and can make gains just by being who you are.

8 TUESDAY   *Moon Age Day 22   Moon Sign Aquarius*

Now you are looking for something bigger, better and brighter. A fast pace of events can be expected in your social life and you should also find that you are much luckier than would usually be the case. There are potential gains to be made from being in the right place to profit from random chance – which isn't really random at all.

9 WEDNESDAY   *Moon Age Day 23   Moon Sign Aquarius*

Avoid making snap decisions for a day or two. It's like you to make up your mind instantly but there are reasons why this may not be such a good idea at this juncture. The more you analyse things, the greater is the likelihood that you will get them right first time. A new education process is about to start for some Aquarians.

10 THURSDAY   *Moon Age Day 24   Moon Sign Pisces*

You should be able to put your persuasive powers to good use when it comes to bringing others round to your own point of view. Everyone around you seems to be engaged on some sort of spring clean and it might occur to you that the time is right to dump things that are no longer of any practical use to you.

11 FRIDAY   *Moon Age Day 25   Moon Sign Pisces*

You seem to be extremely creative at the moment and may turn some of this trend in the direction of your home. You know instinctively what looks and feels right and won't take no for an answer when you have made up your mind regarding a specific change. You can be fairly stubborn at the moment, as friends will readily admit.

12 SATURDAY   *Moon Age Day 26   Moon Sign Aries*

Right now a change of scenery would do a great deal to lighten your load in life and you get on best when you are not working all the time. The odd break makes you commit yourself more when you are applying yourself and also gives you some good ideas. Personal freedom is particularly important to Aquarius at present.

13 SUNDAY   *Moon Age Day 27   Moon Sign Aries*

Intimate matters are now centre stage in your life and you may want to sort something out as far as your love life is concerned. You are still likely to be attracting a lot of attention from some rather surprising directions, as well as impressing people at work. This is Aquarius at its best but you do need to slow down from time to time.

14 MONDAY   *Moon Age Day 28   Moon Sign Taurus*

Prepare for some unexpected ups and downs at the start of this week, some of which come along because of the good offices of friends and colleagues. You may not be an especially deep thinker at the moment but you will be bearing in mind the needs of people you care for. They, in return, will be heaping a great deal of affection on you.

15 TUESDAY   *Moon Age Day 0   Moon Sign Taurus*

There are some interesting possibilities likely to come along early in the week but you may feel a little lethargic and not inclined to follow up on them. Take some time out to think things through and clear the decks for action from midweek on. Watch out for a particularly intriguing offer for travel next month.

16 WEDNESDAY   *Moon Age Day 1   Moon Sign Gemini*

Beware of being too rash for your own good. The problem is that you are likely to speak out without thinking much in advance. This could land you in some hot water and you will need to react quickly in order to get out of trouble. Fortunately you are well equipped for thinking on your feet.

17 THURSDAY   *Moon Age Day 2   Moon Sign Gemini*

Much of May shows you to be less family-motivated than might sometimes be the case and you seem to be getting a great deal from friends, one or two of whom are making a return visit to your life. Many of the values you hold in common with others display themselves in quite a marked manner at present.

18 FRIDAY   *Moon Age Day 3   Moon Sign Cancer*

It looks as though you will have to deal with some restlessness that is rising within your nature at present. Staying put and concentrating on the same old things won't appeal to you at all. It could be the arrival of the early summer or simply a few significant planetary trends but whatever the cause you need to move about.

19 SATURDAY   *Moon Age Day 4   Moon Sign Cancer*

A domestic relationship or some situation within your immediate vicinity is likely to become more of an issue today. You will require flexibility and understanding in order to deal well with others and you will need to exhibit a lot of patience. The truth is that nagging doubts you feel today probably have no basis in fact.

20 SUNDAY
Moon Age Day 5   Moon Sign Leo

Changes go on but some of them leave you behind for the next couple of days as the lunar low makes you quieter and much more inclined to retreat into your own little world. Prepare for some fairly inevitable delays and a need to reorganise your plans at the last minute. Some of this could be quite frustrating but your cheerfulness remains.

21 MONDAY
Moon Age Day 6   Moon Sign Leo

Circumstances may still seem to be working against you and it is a fact that you need to be quite circumspect in the way you approach life generally. Not everything that looks unfortunate turns out to be so at all. Disasters are not likely but there could be some genuine embarrassment as a result of something you do quite innocently.

22 TUESDAY
Moon Age Day 7   Moon Sign Leo

When you are faced with something that genuinely interests you it should be easy to race for the finishing line but the same cannot be said of jobs that you see as boring or without purpose. Whenever you can you are likely to leave such things to others but you need to be careful that you are not accused of laziness. If there is something you know you should do, get on and do it.

23 WEDNESDAY
Moon Age Day 8   Moon Sign Virgo

Trends suggest that success will come easily to you today and you will be on form, especially when in company. You should relish the presence of interesting and informative people in your life and will be working hard to achieve specific objectives. Most important of all you find it easier to concentrate now.

24 THURSDAY
Moon Age Day 9   Moon Sign Virgo

It might seem as though certain circumstances are working against your best interests now but this isn't necessarily the case. Look at things from a different angle and try to be both original and inventive. It won't be long before you discover that you can even turn misfortune to your advantage.

25 FRIDAY
Moon Age Day 10   Moon Sign Libra

Don't overestimate your capabilities today and if you know you are somehow out of your depth, this would be a good time to seek some expert advice. You will probably be in the mood for shopping and there are things you will want to get done at home. If you stick to familiar ground this is likely to be a busy but generally rewarding day.

26 SATURDAY
Moon Age Day 11   Moon Sign Libra

Practical issues should be easier to deal with now and you have a great deal of tolerance when dealing with others. Colleagues are likely to be quite demanding but you look to their humanity and will be showing great sensitivity to the needs of others generally. Routines can be a drag but they may be necessary.

27 SUNDAY
Moon Age Day 12   Moon Sign Scorpio

New ideas and altered perspectives are nothing new to the average Aquarian. Today you excel when it comes to looking at alternatives and you carry the opinions of others with you because of your powers of persuasion. Keep in touch with people who may be far away from you at present.

28 MONDAY
Moon Age Day 13   Moon Sign Scorpio

Though optimism might seem to be in abundance, the fact is that you are somewhat hesitant right now. You will discover that you need constant reassurance from others and will be checking the attitude of family members and friends on a very regular basis. Get organised with family obligations.

29 TUESDAY
Moon Age Day 14   Moon Sign Sagittarius

If there is something you want from a friend or a family member this may be the best day of the month to ask them. Not only do you have a good deal of cheek, you are also blessed with strong persuasive powers. Doing favours for others comes quite naturally and you will also be very tidy-minded at present.

30 WEDNESDAY *Moon Age Day 15   Moon Sign Sagittarius*

You are entering a period that has a great deal to offer in a social sense and although you will be applying yourself very well at work, it is those hours you spend away from responsibility that are likely to be the most rewarding. Your energy levels remain especially high and you should be quite sporting in attitude.

31 THURSDAY *Moon Age Day 16   Moon Sign Sagittarius*

Be bold, brave and determined when faced with some sort of challenge. This won't be difficult because you are clearly in the market for stretching yourself – though only when it suits your purposes to do so. You certainly will not take kindly to being told what to do by anyone today.

June 2018

1 FRIDAY
Moon Age Day 17   Moon Sign Capricorn

Exciting social encounters can be expected today. Stay away from what you see as being pointless rules and regulations because these will only annoy you. Friends should prove to be both supportive and very interesting as the day wears on. You have a lot of strength now and you will not retreat from any kind of challenge.

2 SATURDAY
Moon Age Day 18   Moon Sign Capricorn

Aquarius can be the life and soul of the party at the moment. Although you might not be making the forward strides you would wish in the workplace, you will be able to compensate for this by using your natural charm. Bulldozing your way through any obstacle really is not necessary at this time.

3 SUNDAY
Moon Age Day 19   Moon Sign Aquarius

You should be able to accomplish a great deal today. There are strong planetary forces on your side, even apart from the lunar high. Now is the time to identify what you want from life and then to go out and get it. Gathering support for any cause close to your heart should be child's play at present.

4 MONDAY
Moon Age Day 20   Moon Sign Aquarius

Your attention may well be turned towards financial matters today. Expect better than average success early in the day, though there may be something of a temporary decline from the middle of the afternoon onwards. The good trends of the lunar high dominate though, so the means to enjoy yourself is presently second nature.

5 TUESDAY *Moon Age Day 21   Moon Sign Aquarius*

A heavily competitive element comes along now, forcing you to look at even existing circumstances in a radically different way. You won't want to lose at any game or sport, whilst in terms of career prospects your mind is working overtime. All the same, find a few hours to enjoy yourself.

6 WEDNESDAY *Moon Age Day 22   Moon Sign Pisces*

Despite your best efforts, it could appear that you are missing out somehow in the career stakes and you feel overlooked at work. This would be an ideal time for a reappraisal. If necessary, seek out some professional advice and certainly don't assume that you already know the answer to any problem.

7 THURSDAY *Moon Age Day 23   Moon Sign Pisces*

Success comes at the moment partly through being well organised. You can fall down only if you haven't dealt with all possible eventualities. Don't let opportunities slip by simply because you haven't prepared yourself properly. This would be a good time to instigate new business partnerships.

8 FRIDAY *Moon Age Day 24   Moon Sign Aries*

This should be a very productive day and one that might easily lead to better recognition of your talents from people in your environment. Concentrate on the task at hand and avoid allowing yourself to become diverted by situations that don't really need your special touch at all. It is very important to remain focused now.

9 SATURDAY *Moon Age Day 25   Moon Sign Aries*

In relationships, you are not as friendly and giving today as has been the case recently. Maybe it is the more competitive side of your nature that is on display but for one reason or another it is harder to get close to certain important people. With the weekend here you might opt for a change of scenery.

10 SUNDAY
Moon Age Day 26   Moon Sign Aries

Matters should proceed very much according to plan today, which could mean you aren't a vital part of their workings; all the more reason to get out of the house and to go somewhere interesting. You are a cultured type, so perhaps you could visit a historic ruin, or take a long walk in a scenic place.

11 MONDAY
Moon Age Day 27   Moon Sign Taurus

There is plenty of energy present at the moment to allow you to break through barriers that might have looked high and wide indeed in the recent past. Once you have done so, you might be left wondering why you were intimidated in the first place and you will definitely be sharpening your persuasive skills and general intellect today.

12 TUESDAY
Moon Age Day 28   Moon Sign Taurus

Try to keep things on an even keel at work and avoid allowing yourself to become distracted by matters you cannot control. Be prepared to accept some timely help and advice, especially when it comes from the direction of someone you care about deeply. Confronting certain issues might not work too well today.

13 WEDNESDAY
Moon Age Day 0   Moon Sign Gemini

You can expect an eventful social life, together with constantly improving trends in deeper attachments. Aquarians who are now just starting a new romantic relationship are likely to find it going from strength to strength. When decisions have to be made, use your strong intuition.

14 THURSDAY
Moon Age Day 1   Moon Sign Gemini

There are plenty of opportunities to hog the limelight, though you may be tiring of having to smile so much. You won't be stuck for an answer and this is definitely the best time to put yourself on display. If there are any limitations on you during present trends, these are probably self-created.

15 FRIDAY   *Moon Age Day 2   Moon Sign Cancer*

It is possible that you will discover other people's true feelings about you around this time. In the main, you ought to be delighted but your ego can easily be dented if not all responses are exactly what you would wish. You have to come to terms with the fact that not everyone loves you.

16 SATURDAY   *Moon Age Day 3   Moon Sign Cancer*

Where affairs of the heart are concerned trends should be much improved at the moment. For some there will be brand new romantic interests around and you certainly have what it takes to impress people. However, you should stick to routines at work and don't try anything new or outrageous.

17 SUNDAY   *Moon Age Day 4   Moon Sign Leo*

Though your dealings with others in social settings could be somewhat strained, there are those amongst your friends who rate you highly. Practically speaking, this is a time of high achievement. Avoid unnecessary discussions about situations that don't interest you and which you cannot alter.

18 MONDAY   *Moon Age Day 5   Moon Sign Leo*

Put any major issues on the back burner and prepare yourself for a day or two that could easily turn out to be quiet. This is no bad thing and will allow you some time to think about yourself and projects you are presently planning. Although you may not feel highly charged in a social sense, there are offers about.

19 TUESDAY   *Moon Age Day 6   Moon Sign Virgo*

Your home life should be fairly comfortable at this time and you will be doing all you can to please those with whom you live. Although this might not be turning out to be the most exciting week you have ever lived through it does seem to have a high degree of certainty about it and that can be gratifying.

20 WEDNESDAY   *Moon Age Day 7   Moon Sign Virgo*

Today is still good for any form of contemplation and for mulling over situations that you know you are going to have to deal with before very long. Put some hard work and effort into finding answers that lie deep within your own nature. Your confidence remains steady but you won't need to be making any waves now.

21 THURSDAY   *Moon Age Day 8   Moon Sign Libra*

The best thing you can do for yourself at the moment is to keep busy. Your financial potential looks especially good and you should be able to push forward strongly with new plans. Although you might not be able to do too much today with regard to work, you will be champing at the bit to get on with things generally.

22 FRIDAY   *Moon Age Day 9   Moon Sign Libra*

Good ideas can now be turned into profit, simply by following them through. This might require the support of others but you won't be short of influence at this time and can certainly make almost anyone follow your lead. Romance shines out as being very significant in your life throughout today.

23 SATURDAY   *Moon Age Day 10   Moon Sign Scorpio*

There can be a slight lack of consideration all round at the beginning of this weekend and as a result you might find one or two spats developing. Of course you will want to have your say but there isn't really much point in arguing. It may be a case of leaving people to get on with it, whilst you do something very different.

24 SUNDAY   *Moon Age Day 11   Moon Sign Scorpio*

You can look towards the past with a very nostalgic attitude at the moment but it isn't all that clear how much use this state of mind will be to you. In another way you remain progressive and might grow slightly frustrated if you spend too much time mulling over what has been. Continued commitment is what really counts.

25 MONDAY   *Moon Age Day 12   Moon Sign Scorpio*

You might be better off thinking about solo pursuits now and won't want to be mixing quite as freely with others as has been the case of late. If you can't get a particular job completely finished right now, don't worry. There will be time enough later to deal with the final touches.

26 TUESDAY   *Moon Age Day 13   Moon Sign Sagittarius*

Professional matters are looking fortunate, but that isn't really much help to Aquarians who are presently enjoying a more social interlude. Practical matters remain on your mind and you won't be as able to relax as you might wish. Avoid situations that mean having to confront those you care for.

27 WEDNESDAY   *Moon Age Day 14   Moon Sign Sagittarius*

You seem to have a particularly good insight into many matters at the moment and this can be turned to your practical advantage. Life doesn't seem to need all that much planning or effort and situations will probably be going very much your way. Follow your natural instincts when dealing with younger people or family members.

28 THURSDAY   *Moon Age Day 15   Moon Sign Capricorn*

A proposal that comes your way at the moment should be treated with caution and you should not sign any documents without looking at the small print very carefully. Allow others to take some of the decisions today but not if they are really important ones. Tomorrow is another day and should look more positive.

29 FRIDAY   *Moon Age Day 16   Moon Sign Capricorn*

A more intellectual element appears in your chart, particularly connected with personal attachments. You may find you have something in common with your partner or sweetheart that you never realised before. For some this can open up another world. In a general sense, you can get what you want socially, which matters a lot now.

30 SATURDAY   *Moon Age Day 17   Moon Sign Capricorn*

The course of true love ought to be running very smoothly for most Aquarians at the moment and this is a Saturday during which you are able to demonstrate your affection very well indeed. The attitude of some friends can be baffling but just leave them to settle down before you react too strongly.

July

2018

1 SUNDAY
Moon Age Day 18   Moon Sign Aquarius

The time comes along for a completely confident approach, assisted greatly by the presence of the Moon in your own zodiac sign. If there are things you are bursting to say, now is the time. With more than your fair share of good luck at this time, you can afford to chance your arm a little more than usual.

2 MONDAY
Moon Age Day 19   Moon Sign Aquarius

The good times should be continuing, probably despite a little news that looks less than favourable initially. Stay away from boring jobs and be out there in the wide world as much as possible today. The more you mix and mingle, the greater will be your ability to make friends and influence others.

3 TUESDAY
Moon Age Day 20   Moon Sign Pisces

Make the most of beneficial highlights that come along, particularly at work. Good results come from practical efforts and you have what it takes to make the most of all situations today. Love and romance are principle amongst your concerns today and you should find popularity amongst your peers.

4 WEDNESDAY
Moon Age Day 21   Moon Sign Pisces

Personal contact with co-workers looks as if it is going to turn out better today than has been the case for quite some time. It could be that some sort of antagonism has been evident and it is now possible to put that behind you. Friends should be disarming and especially warm right now.

5 THURSDAY
Moon Age Day 22   Moon Sign Pisces

The current planetary focus is on work and you are kept very much on the move today, whether or not you are actually holding down a position at the moment. Socially speaking you seem content to have a good time, though there is a quieter side to your nature that shows itself occasionally at present.

6 FRIDAY
Moon Age Day 23   Moon Sign Aries

When it comes to fulfilling the expectations that others have of you, the chances are that you are second to none right now. Convincing others of your sincerity in almost any situation should not be at all difficult. Get some rest if you have been burning the candle at both ends, though without killing your social life stone dead.

7 SATURDAY
Moon Age Day 24   Moon Sign Aries

Beware because you might be up against some strident views, most of which are coming from the direction of people you associate with on a day-to-day basis. Take life steadily today and don't allow yourself to become flustered by issues that normally would not bother you in the slightest.

8 SUNDAY
Moon Age Day 25   Moon Sign Taurus

At work you could be a winner, and this positive trend is set to last for a while. This is only really relevant if you are a weekend worker, otherwise you will be putting your efforts into your home and social life. Trends also suggest that concern for the underdog is high in the list of Aquarian priorities at this point in time.

9 MONDAY
Moon Age Day 26   Moon Sign Taurus

You should enjoy social discussions of almost any sort now. Concern for others is still strong though it is likely that family members are faring better now than seems to have been the case for the last few days. At work you are aware that there is no shortcut to success, so simply keep ploughing on regardless.

10 TUESDAY *Moon Age Day 27   Moon Sign Gemini*

Positive highlights in relationships can make this a very good day on the personal front. At the same time you are overtaken by a distinctly nostalgic mood, one that can take your mind far back into the past. A strong boost to social matters, together with progressive trends, might also turn your mind towards sport.

11 WEDNESDAY *Moon Age Day 28   Moon Sign Gemini*

A variety of new interests now allow you to get the very best from life. Try not to get overanxious about situations that don't really matter at all. Cultivate your more creative side and seek out intellectual stimulation. Soap operas and computer games won't offer you as much as cultural pursuits right now so look for a diversion from your usual life.

12 THURSDAY *Moon Age Day 29   Moon Sign Cancer*

A variety of different sorts of news and views should be coming your way at this stage of the working week. You have plenty of confidence when you need it the most but you will have to work especially hard for something you have definitely set your mind on having. Conforming to the expectations others have of you isn't always easy now.

13 FRIDAY *Moon Age Day 0   Moon Sign Cancer*

This is a time when, on the whole, things do go better in pairs. In a general sense you know what you want from life, but others may have a better idea than you do how to go about getting it. Don't play dangerous games with friendship though. A straight bat and an honest approach are always the best for you.

14 SATURDAY *Moon Age Day 1   Moon Sign Leo*

A lull patch commences with the arrival of the lunar low. Although you are hardly likely to feel depressed during such a generally positive time in your life, there will be some setbacks if you insist on keeping up your general speed. Create a little space for yourself today and having done so – sit in it and relax.

15 SUNDAY   *Moon Age Day 2   Moon Sign Leo*

Although another day that is less than inspiring, this Sunday shows you to have slightly more influence than was probably the case yesterday. Friends should be willing to help you out and have some interesting news to impart when it matters the most. Slowly but surely, you climb out of your little quiet spell.

16 MONDAY   *Moon Age Day 3   Moon Sign Virgo*

You now find yourself in a period during which all practical matters should push ahead quite nicely. Difficulties associated with relationships are less likely at this time and you can rely on friends to offer the sort of support you need, when you want it the most. This should be a good start to the week.

17 TUESDAY   *Moon Age Day 4   Moon Sign Virgo*

Your good ideas and ingenuity are called into play this week. People you might never have imagined would be interested in listening to your views will be sounding you out now and can easily offer you something in return. Romance looks fine too, perhaps with a surprise or two on the way.

18 WEDNESDAY   *Moon Age Day 5   Moon Sign Libra*

There is a definite tendency towards acquisition at this time of the week and this might cause you to focus on the wrong things. Whilst you can make money in one way, it is likely to be slipping through your fingers in others. Your confidence remains intact but the days ahead could call for a more concentrated approach.

19 THURSDAY   *Moon Age Day 6   Moon Sign Libra*

Socialising is good today, though not if you allow yourself to get involved in disputes that shouldn't be taking place at all. Try to stay neutral if possible, even playing the arbitrator amongst arguing friends. The events now are interesting but you have to steer a careful course if you don't want to become involved.

20 FRIDAY
Moon Age Day 7   Moon Sign Libra

There are dangers right now in trying to make the world run the way you wish. It would be far better for the moment to realise that your own opinions belong to you and that others may not share them. Mistakes will be made today but you are good at putting forward a loss limitation exercise.

21 SATURDAY
Moon Age Day 8   Moon Sign Scorpio

When it comes to getting what you want, you are king of the castle this weekend. Of all the weeks of July, this one should be potentially the best. Although you might find it difficult to understand what makes loved ones tick, you are not having anywhere near the same problem with either colleagues or friends.

22 SUNDAY
Moon Age Day 9   Moon Sign Scorpio

Material gains were never going to be far away during a period in which you are registering so many personal successes. Your confidence remains high and now you become something of a diplomat. Warring parties in any sphere of your life are treated to a dose of your ability to act as arbitrator.

23 MONDAY
Moon Age Day 10   Moon Sign Sagittarius

You are out to impress people today and it won't be hard to do so. It might not be easy to conform to the expectations of others, mainly because you are a born original in the first place. Your creative potential is good and you might spend at least part of today somehow brightening up your home surroundings.

24 TUESDAY
Moon Age Day 11   Moon Sign Sagittarius

Your mind is of the quick-fire variety today and you won't be stuck for an answer, no matter what the question might be. This doesn't mean to say that all your comments are either correct or very clever, but you can fool enough people to get by well enough. A little cheek goes a long way.

25 WEDNESDAY   *Moon Age Day 12*   *Moon Sign Capricorn*

Specific information that comes to you now from colleagues or possibly friends is definitely worth listening to carefully. Don't assume you have all the answers yourself and be willing to admit your limitations. If you ally the skills of those around you to your own the sky is the limit.

26 THURSDAY   *Moon Age Day 13*   *Moon Sign Capricorn*

Don't take no for an answer in situations about which you are absolutely certain. At the same time, try to use all your diplomatic skills. Bear in mind that not everyone is equally easy to deal with and it would be quite sensible to listen carefully to what others have to say before you speak out.

27 FRIDAY   *Moon Age Day 14*   *Moon Sign Capricorn*

Be open and ready for new input at this time, especially from people who have been trying for some time to become part of your inner circle. Things may be changing somewhat in terms of the people you mix with on a day-to day-basis and there is now a definite feeling of 'off with the old and on with the new'.

28 SATURDAY   *Moon Age Day 15*   *Moon Sign Aquarius*

It's close to the end of the month and the Moon returns to your zodiac sign, leading to a period of high activity and a weekend that revolves around your social life. There might not be all that much time for practicalities but since you have charm galore, you can get others to do the dirty work.

29 SUNDAY   *Moon Age Day 16*   *Moon Sign Aquarius*

There is positive help around when you need it, together with the personally-held view that you know your own business best. The desire for a change of scene could be very strong and is emphasised even more by the lunar high. What an excellent time this would be for Aquarius to take a holiday.

30 MONDAY
Moon Age Day 17   Moon Sign Pisces

What happens in the practical world today could prove to be quite decisive. Maybe you are making significant changes at home, or expecting family members to behave in particular ways. All you are looking at could come to very little unless you make it plain that you have your finger on important pulses.

31 TUESDAY
Moon Age Day 18   Moon Sign Pisces

Even though you know what you are doing, the same cannot be said to be true of people with whom you have to co-operate. It would be sensible to check and double-check almost anything now, particularly documents or work that always requires scrutiny. Aquarius cannot leave anything to chance now.

August 2018

1 WEDNESDAY ☿ *Moon Age Day 19 Moon Sign Pisces*

Some professional requirements can be tricky today and you will have to think them through as carefully as you can. Make sure you are getting enough rest at this time and don't expect more of yourself than is reasonable. There is help there for the taking but you will have to admit you are struggling in order to get it.

2 THURSDAY ☿ *Moon Age Day 20 Moon Sign Aries*

Someone very close to you may well do you a great service today and you will want to find ways and means to pay them back. Attitude is all-important when you are dealing with people who can be difficult. It is essential to remain patient and not to push situations more than is strictly necessary.

3 FRIDAY ☿ *Moon Age Day 21 Moon Sign Aries*

Avoid impulse buying today and only spend money when you know for certain that you are getting a genuine bargain. Don't be too quick to take offence over remarks that probably were not directed at you in any case and be willing to eat humble pie if you do misunderstand what others are saying.

4 SATURDAY ☿ *Moon Age Day 22 Moon Sign Taurus*

Your personal finances could now be rather up and down. Believe it or not, it is possible for you to get by on very little today because you start to realise that money is not everything. But then, just when you have taken this fact on board – along comes some cash you didn't expect.

5 SUNDAY ☿ *Moon Age Day 23* *Moon Sign Taurus*

It's time to get yourself very organised. If you really want to make the best of this period, the stars say that you must think well ahead and act with great decision this Sunday. It might mean taking some things at a slower pace but as long as you are thorough, you should make gains.

6 MONDAY ☿ *Moon Age Day 24* *Moon Sign Gemini*

This is not a day to allow yourself to get down in the dumps about anything. You need to remain sure of yourself and confident in whatever you are doing. Not everything will go your way in the week ahead, but when it really matters you have enough about you to pull out the stops and make things happen.

7 TUESDAY ☿ *Moon Age Day 25* *Moon Sign Gemini*

This is a time when you simply love to be the centre of attention. Don't be surprised if you discover that you have some admirers, and prepare for the fact that it might not be long before one or two of them are making the situation abundantly clear. The only problem is that you might be too naïve to realise.

8 WEDNESDAY ☿ *Moon Age Day 26* *Moon Sign Gemini*

The strong drive to achieve that has been a part of your nature over the last couple of weeks is still intact. You can't have everything you want at present, though you should be in possession of most of what you need. There's a subtle difference, as you will realise if you just stop to think for a while.

9 THURSDAY ☿ *Moon Age Day 27* *Moon Sign Cancer*

Your desire to make important changes won't be without something of a struggle at the moment. Still, it's worth putting in that extra bit of effort if what you get out of it at the end is improvements to your life. Stand by for some promising remarks from individuals who are in an excellent position to offer you a boost.

10 FRIDAY ☿ *Moon Age Day 28   Moon Sign Cancer*

Get things moving in your life this Friday by keeping going, even when others are falling by the wayside. You have a good reserve of energy there when you need it the most, though you won't be averse to putting your feet up either. Financial gains are by no means guaranteed at this time, but they are possible.

11 SATURDAY ☿ *Moon Age Day 0   Moon Sign Leo*

Although this is hardly likely to be your luckiest time, you can help yourself by refusing to get drawn into money-making schemes that you know in your heart are a waste of time. You have confidence in your own ability but that won't be enough on its own to see you through. Perhaps focus on creative matters instead.

12 SUNDAY ☿ *Moon Age Day 1   Moon Sign Leo*

Although you are less dynamic and energetic today than you might wish, that doesn't prevent you from looking ahead and planning your strategies carefully. Be willing to take a break from the rat race and listen to the wise words of people who have more experience in the world than you have yourself.

13 MONDAY ☿ *Moon Age Day 2   Moon Sign Virgo*

Material restrictions may force you to cut back on one or two things, though probably not for long. In a way it doesn't matter because what you want most from life at the moment cannot be purchased with any amount of cash. Your search is for personal happiness and there is a good chance you are going to find it, in part at least.

14 TUESDAY ☿ *Moon Age Day 3   Moon Sign Virgo*

If you want to make the most of present social trends, you have to put in that extra bit of effort that can mean success. What doesn't come easily at present is conforming to the expectations of others. At the end of the day you have to be certain that what you are doing is right for you.

15 WEDNESDAY ☿   *Moon Age Day 4   Moon Sign Libra*

There is wonderful company out there at present. All you have to do is to set out and find it. Keep a sense of proportion when you are dealing with people who have big ideas but perhaps not the follow-through to put them into action. Come to think of it, this may be the start of a stunning double-act.

16 THURSDAY ☿   *Moon Age Day 5   Moon Sign Libra*

Financial planning undertaken now is likely to work out well. You have a very astute head on your shoulders and are also in a good position to see a host of different possibilities and strategies around this time. Aquarius is both confident and comfortable under these trends, and it shows.

17 FRIDAY ☿   *Moon Age Day 6   Moon Sign Scorpio*

Although it is clear you are looking for a high degree of personal freedom right now, you must get important jobs out of the way before you think about taking a break. Don't be inclined to sit on the fence in issues you know to be important. Even if it means disagreeing with a friend, you have to speak your mind.

18 SATURDAY ☿   *Moon Age Day 7   Moon Sign Scorpio*

Joint financial endeavours and co-operative ventures generally are well accented right now. Your intuitive powers are at their peak, allowing you to weigh up any given situation almost instantly. With a slight change of emphasis, people now see you as someone who is good at talking, rather than a contentious person.

19 SUNDAY   *Moon Age Day 8   Moon Sign Sagittarius*

If you had been planning on taking a chance in any romantic sense, now is the time to do it. Winning others round to your point of view, even beyond personal relationships, ought to be quite easy. Fortune favours the brave and you have more than a little courage on show for much of the coming week.

20 MONDAY   *Moon Age Day 9   Moon Sign Sagittarius*

You will want to deal with practical issues as quickly as you can, maybe because there are things to do that are simply for the sake of enjoyment. Don't feel guilty about this. Few people could put in more effort than you have across the last couple of weeks, so it is only fair that you also take some time to yourself.

21 TUESDAY   *Moon Age Day 10   Moon Sign Sagittarius*

Things are likely to be well on course and there is every chance you could find some special moments today. If you suddenly realise there is a job you should have done that is still waiting, now is the time to get cracking. Your capacity for work is very good at the moment and you have great staying power.

22 WEDNESDAY   *Moon Age Day 11   Moon Sign Capricorn*

Do more of your own thing today, and don't worry about pleasing others all the time. This isn't really selfish, and even if it could be considered so, remember that you do have the right to address your own life sometimes. Avoid family disputes, especially since you are not the one who is starting them.

23 THURSDAY   *Moon Age Day 12   Moon Sign Capricorn*

Today could turn out to be a good deal more exciting than you expected. If you are working look out for a chance to gain new power or responsibilities. However, if you have the day to yourself, think about making changes to your social life and maybe even taking a few small, calculated risks.

24 FRIDAY   *Moon Age Day 13   Moon Sign Aquarius*

Now comes the chance to put longed-for plans and ambitions to the test. This is very much your day but how it goes depends entirely on the amount of effort you are willing to put in. That won't be a problem at all because you are raring to go. Try to be quite cool, even on those occasions when you are very nervous inside.

25 SATURDAY   *Moon Age Day 14   Moon Sign Aquarius*

Put your persuasive powers to the test and ask for what you want. With a little cheek and very good communication skills it is highly unlikely that anyone will refuse your reasonable requests. Money matters ought to be better and there is even the possibility of a small windfall at some stage during the day.

26 SUNDAY   *Moon Age Day 15   Moon Sign Aquarius*

Certain friendships have a lot going for them at the moment and these are the ones on which you need to concentrate the most. Don't betray any confidences, especially when you know how upset certain parties would be if you did. You can't trust certain people to keep their mouths shut.

27 MONDAY   *Moon Age Day 16   Moon Sign Pisces*

There is a continued accent on work and material considerations today, so much so that you might find it difficult to spend any time doing exactly what you want. When you do have free hours, you are likely to spend a good proportion of them supporting other people, particularly friends who are having difficulties.

28 TUESDAY   *Moon Age Day 17   Moon Sign Pisces*

Practical situations demand your attention much more than usual now and it is a fact that you won't have as much time today to concentrate on personal issues, or the concerns of your friends. Avoid getting yourself into something of a panic now by pacing yourself and resisting the urge to take on too much.

29 WEDNESDAY   *Moon Age Day 18   Moon Sign Aries*

Getting along with others should be very easy as today gets started. It isn't usually difficult for you in any case, though there have been a few occasions in the recent past when you haven't been quite as accommodating as usual. Bear in mind that some tasks may have to be spread out in order to get them done properly.

30 THURSDAY   *Moon Age Day 19   Moon Sign Aries*

What you hear from others can be of great use to you at present, so it is definitely worthwhile keeping your ears open today. That shouldn't be too much of a problem because Aquarius is one of the best dealers in gossip to be found anywhere within the zodiac. Look out for small financial gains.

31 FRIDAY   *Moon Age Day 20   Moon Sign Aries*

This might be a period of time during which you will want to restructure elements of your life that you feel are not going the way you would wish. Instead of spending too much money today, plan how you can get more. The time for spoiling yourself comes later but for now you really need to work hard.

September 2018

1 SATURDAY
Moon Age Day 21   Moon Sign Taurus

It appears that you are not in control of certain major personal issues in your life, or at least that is how it is going to seem at the moment. There is no shame in seeking some timely advice, specifically from people who know a great deal about your life and circumstances. New friends are on the cards soon.

2 SUNDAY
Moon Age Day 22   Moon Sign Taurus

Your chart suggests that you might be retreating somewhat from the more frenetic qualities of life, but this appears to be only as a temporary trend. With all to play for socially and romantically, drop the traces of responsibility in order to enjoy yourself in some leisurely pursuits today. The break will do you good.

3 MONDAY
Moon Age Day 23   Moon Sign Gemini

The first day of the working week brings professional developments for many and probably finds you in a very innovative frame of mind. You are able to get your head round matters that could have been quite confusing before and will probably kick yourself for not having more savvy previously.

4 TUESDAY
Moon Age Day 24   Moon Sign Gemini

Perhaps this isn't the best of times to gamble, particularly when it comes to games of chance that leave you little chance of winning anything. However, when you are faced with a certainty you should follow it all the way. When assessing the way others will behave you can now afford to use your intuition.

5 WEDNESDAY — *Moon Age Day 25   Moon Sign Cancer*

The more determined edge to your nature returns in no uncertain terms. When it comes to getting things right first time, you should have no problem at all. Your confidence is on the increase again and is assisted by the present position of the Sun in your solar eighth house. This is still a transitional period for you.

6 THURSDAY — *Moon Age Day 26   Moon Sign Cancer*

Minor financial gains are possible, though probably as a result of your own efforts rather than as a result of any good luck. Once again you discover that, having made a decision, you are inclined to stick to it, even at the expense of common sense. Doing things your own way is more or less an art form for Aquarius now.

7 FRIDAY — *Moon Age Day 27   Moon Sign Leo*

It's time to slow the action and to take stock. The lunar low this time doesn't bring much in the way of bad luck, or even a less than favourable frame of mind. What it does bestow is the chance to look at matters again, but this time with the addition of more common sense and circumspection.

8 SATURDAY — *Moon Age Day 28   Moon Sign Leo*

This could be another less that dynamic day, but once again you discover that you are pensive and able to take stock of situations. Friends ought to be quite helpful now and might be making suggestions that are of specific importance to your longer-term future. It's worth listening to well meant advice.

9 SUNDAY — *Moon Age Day 0   Moon Sign Virgo*

Present planetary trends bring out the detective in you. Finding out what makes people tick is especially interesting at the moment, though you need to take a little care because you don't want to be accused of prying into people's lives. Your creative potential is going off the scale, especially regarding changes at home.

10 MONDAY
Moon Age Day 1   Moon Sign Virgo

Most of the changes occurring in your personal life at present come because you are specifically looking for them. This is a time when it is necessary to peer at old matters in a very new light. All the same you might be left with the impression that you are tinkering with life rather than changing it completely.

11 TUESDAY
Moon Age Day 2   Moon Sign Libra

Your life now contains elements of the weird and wonderful. Bearing in mind what Aquarius is like for much of the time, it is slightly hard to know how you would recognise the difference! All the same, put yourself in the path of new experiences and don't take anything at face value.

12 WEDNESDAY
Moon Age Day 3   Moon Sign Libra

With travel matters positively highlighted in your chart, you should be happily on the go and probably feeling rather less stressed than has been the case of late. Although you have been enjoying life to the full, you may have been putting yourself through the mill too much. Now you can relax more, which has to be good.

13 THURSDAY
Moon Age Day 4   Moon Sign Scorpio

This is another good day for enjoying the great sense of personal freedom that surrounds you at present. Travel takes on an importance that could extend into your professional life, though moving about for its own sake can be fun too. Avoid arguing with people who clearly know their onions.

14 FRIDAY
Moon Age Day 5   Moon Sign Scorpio

This may be a day when your power to bring about significant changes, particularly in your professional life, is very limited. Keep trying though because you will win through in the end. Talking to interesting people should appeal, as will getting out of boring routines and into new situations.

15 SATURDAY   *Moon Age Day 6   Moon Sign Scorpio*

Professional obligations could test your patience if you are a weekend worker. If not, find ways to enjoy yourself beyond the confines of your own front door. The world looks inviting and you should not be short of ideas when it comes to innovation. People will find you good to have around.

16 SUNDAY   *Moon Age Day 7   Moon Sign Sagittarius*

Now you are able to catch up on unfinished business. Sunday allows you more time to please yourself and to look at things in a new and innovative way. You may be concerned for the underdog, and you are especially good at sorting out the needs and wants of younger family members. Your confidence is on the increase again.

17 MONDAY   *Moon Age Day 8   Moon Sign Sagittarius*

This might be a good time to look at the way your life is structured and a period for making necessary changes. It's late in the year for a spring clean but that is more or less what seems to be happening. Don't keep hold of anything simply for the sake of habit. You may have to be slightly ruthless.

18 TUESDAY   *Moon Age Day 9   Moon Sign Capricorn*

Social matters could be somewhat hectic today, though you do stand the chance of happening across enjoyable situations, possibly without planning any of them. This would not be a good time to get involved in arguments, especially those that crop up in your family or immediate friendship circle.

19 WEDNESDAY   *Moon Age Day 10   Moon Sign Capricorn*

If you have any problems today, turn on your intuition and see what it is telling you. Understanding what makes other people tick should be quite easy and you can achieve some real gains as a result. You are very sympathetic at present and would be quite willing to change your own direction in life a little in order to help someone else.

20 THURSDAY   *Moon Age Day 11   Moon Sign Aquarius*

The Moon moves into your zodiac sign, giving you all the opportunity you need for a really positive day. Not only will you find you are more popular amongst your friends, but family members have wonderful things to say about you, too. Most important of all, you know how to have fun and to inspire it in others.

21 FRIDAY   *Moon Age Day 12   Moon Sign Aquarius*

Personal matters take on an importance during the second day of your lunar high this month. It appears that your level of popularity is high and new romantic encounters, if that's what you're looking for, certainly cannot be ruled out. Your strength of character shows in practically everything you do today.

22 SATURDAY   *Moon Age Day 13   Moon Sign Aquarius*

You could do a lot worse today than spreading your wings. Travel hasn't been uppermost in the mind of Aquarians as much this year as is sometimes the case, but you should find that wanderlust does begin to play a part in your thinking from now on. This would be an ideal time to take an autumn holiday.

23 SUNDAY   *Moon Age Day 14   Moon Sign Pisces*

Now you could discover a period of change coming upon you. It is possible that one or two friendships have run their course. You don't want to hurt anyone, so you simply retreat from situations you now find boring. Some sort of explanation may be called for, even if you have to bend the truth slightly.

24 MONDAY   *Moon Age Day 15   Moon Sign Pisces*

Pressures can come thick and fast at work, though most of them are dismissed with a shrug. Even when you have managed to climb a series of mountains to get what you want from life, further peaks are in view. It is possible you are trying just a little too hard and that you would benefit from a reduction in pace.

25 TUESDAY   *Moon Age Day 16   Moon Sign Aries*

Emotional matters tend to get quite intense today and you need to be careful not to get involved in any rows. It might appear that people you are usually close to are singularly failing to understand or fall in line with your point of view. A dollop of respect all round seems to be necessary.

26 WEDNESDAY   *Moon Age Day 17   Moon Sign Aries*

Get out and about if you can, the further the better. You might be quieter than usual but would fare better if visiting places you haven't seen before. Likewise, you may find strangers easier to get along with than people you have known for a long time. This may also be a period for puzzles of one sort or another.

27 THURSDAY   *Moon Age Day 18   Moon Sign Aries*

Financial matters could make life seem very secure. There may be more cash about than would often be the case, some of it likely to come from rather unexpected directions. Conforming to expectations could be rather difficult and you won't relish routine tasks, which you see as being very boring at present.

28 FRIDAY   *Moon Age Day 19   Moon Sign Taurus*

The pace of everyday events goes up a notch or two and you should find some exciting events coming along, even if you have to manufacture at least some of these yourself. At times today your mind is dragged towards the past, either by events or individuals you haven't seen for ages.

29 SATURDAY   *Moon Age Day 20   Moon Sign Taurus*

The start of the weekend would make a fine period for pleasure trips and tends to be quite a nostalgic time too. In terms of work, if you are there today, you may be able to close a circle in some way and it does look as if new starts with alternative responsibilities are coming along for many Aquarians.

30 SUNDAY
Moon Age Day 21   Moon Sign Gemini

Hopeful news could be coming your way from far off places. Any Aquarian who has been looking forward to a long journey may not have to wait much longer. There are gains to be made from family members, some of whom are coming up with extremely good and innovative ideas at present.

October

2018

1 MONDAY
Moon Age Day 22   Moon Sign Gemini

Mundane matters are apt to get in the way of your personal freedom today, so make sure that your point of view is still being heard and that you don't allow the general pace of your life to obscure specific issues. Other trends in your chart suggest that romance is on the cards for some Aquarians at this point in time.

2 TUESDAY
Moon Age Day 23   Moon Sign Cancer

Trends favourably highlight communication issues now making it clear that you intend to speak to as many people as possible today in your efforts to get ahead generally. There are few barriers in your way when it comes to getting your message across intact and, in the main others want to help you if they can.

3 WEDNESDAY
Moon Age Day 24   Moon Sign Cancer

Along comes an opportunity to broaden your horizons in ways that you may not have thought of before. Grasp the nettle firmly and take the chance to push your influence with others. If you have some grandiose new scheme it is definitely time to get others on your side and you have the skills to do so.

4 THURSDAY
Moon Age Day 25   Moon Sign Leo

Getting ahead quite as easily as you may wish isn't going to be easy with the lunar low around. Why try? This Thursday offers you the perfect opportunity to sit and watch life go by for a while. You will feel much better if you take a break and will then be well equipped to make use of favourable trends later on.

5 FRIDAY
Moon Age Day 26   Moon Sign Leo

This is not necessarily a period of self-gain, but it really depends on the way you approach certain situations. Go slow and steady, weighing up the pros and cons in each case. The more carefully you address the fine details, the greater is the likelihood of success in the end.

6 SATURDAY
Moon Age Day 27   Moon Sign Virgo

Although you cannot please all of the people, all of the time, there's a good chance you will get close to doing so. The fact is that you are as charming as can be right now, something that others could hardly fail to register. Some jobs will take a good deal longer than you expected but it is simply a matter of carrying on steadily.

7 SUNDAY
Moon Age Day 28   Moon Sign Virgo

A few technical matters have to be ignored today if you want to get ahead quickly. Of course, it would be madness not to take stock of safety issues and you realise this instinctively. It is red tape that bothers you most of all but it appears that you have discovered ways to do something about it.

8 MONDAY
Moon Age Day 29   Moon Sign Virgo

Getting down to brass tacks in your conversations with other people is absolutely vital at this time. There is absolutely no point at the moment in being so diplomatic that those around you fail to understand completely what you are trying to say. Fortunately, there is a middle path that you can usually locate.

9 TUESDAY
Moon Age Day 0   Moon Sign Libra

Although it is clear that you enjoy seeking out the new and unusual in any matter today, in the main you are somewhat hampered by events well beyond your own control. It might be easier in some situations to go with the flow, though that is hardly what typical Aquarian behaviour is all about.

136

10 WEDNESDAY   *Moon Age Day 1   Moon Sign Libra*

It appears that circumstances are conspiring to offer you much more control over your own destiny at this time. That has to be good and you won't be short of ideas. There have been some restrictions on your movement this month but these tend to be lifted now, offering you the chance to travel more.

11 THURSDAY   *Moon Age Day 2   Moon Sign Scorpio*

Socially speaking it seems that you are more reluctant than usual and that you won't necessarily take the initiative at any stage this week. It may be that you are simply regrouping your efforts and waiting for the right chance to push forward positively. On the other hand, you could simply be feeling a bit lazy.

12 FRIDAY   *Moon Age Day 3   Moon Sign Scorpio*

There are matters in the outside world that appear to keep you pretty much in the dark for the moment. Although you will be doing your very best to establish what is really going on, you may simply have to exercise some temporary patience and wait to see what happens in the fullness of time. That isn't easy for you.

13 SATURDAY   *Moon Age Day 4   Moon Sign Sagittarius*

You can now see more light at the end of the tunnel when it comes to getting your own way in social and personal matters. Previously difficult people will see your point of view readily and the host of tasks before you seems to diminish rapidly. Aim for a social weekend and one that offers significant movement.

14 SUNDAY   *Moon Age Day 5   Moon Sign Sagittarius*

Sunday brings a state of affairs that shows little self-control on your part. An ill-disciplined approach to almost anything is not going to help at this time. On the contrary, if you don't keep a close eye on circumstances, a few of them are likely to run out of control so get your act together and take stock.

15 MONDAY   *Moon Age Day 6   Moon Sign Capricorn*

The work-hard/play-hard ethos of your sign is definitely on display right now. Concentrate on those matters that are really important to your future and whenever possible integrate your career and social life. There ought to be ample opportunity once again to make an extremely good impression.

16 TUESDAY   *Moon Age Day 7   Moon Sign Capricorn*

You may need the bright lights of the social world to cheer you up today. There are a number of astrological reasons to explain why you are slightly down in the dumps, though there is no real reason to let these spoil your day. Keep in the mainstream at work and avoid unnecessary controversy.

17 WEDNESDAY   *Moon Age Day 8   Moon Sign Capricorn*

If anything, you are being slightly less consistent today, a good indication that you are not firing on all cylinders. Perhaps you need to look at certain matters more carefully and it would help to keep quiet about them until you have done so. There are gains to be made, though you may have to look hard to find them.

18 THURSDAY   *Moon Age Day 9   Moon Sign Aquarius*

New decisions and initiatives should be cropping up all the time now that the lunar high is with you. Your creative potential is especially good and leads you to understand that everything can go your way with a little effort. General good luck is always increased at this time, so use this fact to your advantage.

19 FRIDAY   *Moon Age Day 10   Moon Sign Aquarius*

You may still be in the running for some good luck as today gets underway. It is worth trying that bit harder to get what you want at work and to persuade other people generally that your point of view is sound and valid. Socially speaking, you may choose not to mix with people if you hear that others are avoiding them.

20 SATURDAY
Moon Age Day 11   Moon Sign Pisces

Some skilful manoeuvring may be necessary if you want to avoid family members falling out with each other. Although you won't necessarily make much material progress today, your ability to sort out the problems of those around you should be pleasing enough in its own right.

21 SUNDAY
Moon Age Day 12   Moon Sign Pisces

This would be a good day to be on the move and to be saying what you think, especially about practical situations. The real gains today might well be romantic. New relationships should be working well under prevailing trends, while established ones seem to have new zest and vitality that you are bringing to them.

22 MONDAY
Moon Age Day 13   Moon Sign Pisces

The best advice that can be offered to Aquarius today is to ensure that you get one task out of the way before you start on another. There is a danger of overlap and confusion that you could so easily avoid. There ought to be a good deal of happiness about in a family and friendship sense.

23 TUESDAY
Moon Age Day 14   Moon Sign Aries

Your desire to please others might fall flat but that is no reason to avoid trying. The area of life that works best for you appears to be that of romance. Finding the right words to say 'I love you' should be quite easy now and the response you get will make the effort more than worthwhile.

24 WEDNESDAY
Moon Age Day 15   Moon Sign Aries

This is not a day during which you should take anything for granted. Check and double check, that's the secret. There are people around who may not appear to have your best interests at heart, though it would be sensible to check the situation out before you fly off the handle.

25 THURSDAY   *Moon Age Day 16   Moon Sign Taurus*

You could find the opinions of others to be either irrelevant or even downright annoying now. It is important not to react too strongly so keep your cool. It is possible for you to achieve some singular successes simply by staying cool and refusing to rise to any bait that is presently offered.

26 FRIDAY   *Moon Age Day 17   Moon Sign Taurus*

Matters in your career should now be looking good. If you are in full time education, expect some good marks and compliments from tutors. Home-based activities could be slightly less than appealing, though you might have to turn your mind in that direction, if only to please your loved ones.

27 SATURDAY   *Moon Age Day 18   Moon Sign Gemini*

Improved communication is likely to be the best gift of the weekend. Don't be tardy when it comes to expressing an opinion, even when you know there are people around who will not agree with you. Although you won't be feeling absolutely positive about everything, you can fool others and even yourself in the end.

28 SUNDAY   *Moon Age Day 19   Moon Sign Gemini*

Although you may not be at work today, the very best astrological trends appear to be pointing in that direction. For this reason, Aquarians who work on a Sunday score highest on the planetary scale today. At home, you may find some of the things that are happening to be tedious and maybe even pointless. Look for fulfilment where you would not usually expect to find it.

29 MONDAY   *Moon Age Day 20   Moon Sign Cancer*

With excellent focus and concentration, you should be looking towards the most distant horizon in your life with enthusiasm. Prepare for a little frustration arising from people who rush ahead and do things without checking, which could lead to a few problems for you further down the line.

30 TUESDAY   *Moon Age Day 21   Moon Sign Cancer*

Don't be dissuaded from doing things your own way. If you put yourself out too much to accommodate the ideas of others, no matter how close they may be, you could be in for a loss of some sort. When your intuition tells you to take a specific course of action it would be sensible to heed it.

31 WEDNESDAY   *Moon Age Day 22   Moon Sign Cancer*

The potential for getting what you want across the board is strong today. There are people around who actively want to offer you help and support and you should be able to locate them easily enough. Conforming to the expectations that older relatives have of you could be somewhat complicated.

November 2018

1 THURSDAY
Moon Age Day 23   Moon Sign Leo

The lunar low brings a planetary lull, just in time for Thursday morning. How this bears on your life really depends on your attitude. As long as you are willing to take comfort in small things, and can shelve some of your most grandiose schemes for just a couple of days, all should be well.

2 FRIDAY
Moon Age Day 24   Moon Sign Leo

The day is here to settle for smaller, less demanding plans. Friday should bring feelings of peace and contentment, together with a willingness to listen to what other people are saying. You could find that the lunar low this time around has turned out to be a blessing in disguise.

3 SATURDAY
Moon Age Day 25   Moon Sign Virgo

Although you could be rather impatient with material obligations today, you will have to get these out of the way before you can begin to move forward in certain respects. It isn't so much what people need of you that can irritate, more what some of them expect. It is very important to keep your cool.

4 SUNDAY
Moon Age Day 26   Moon Sign Virgo

Being on the move can be quite rewarding. This is certainly not a time to be standing still or to allow the grass to grow under your feet with regard to exciting new plans. You will be amazed just how much work you can get through right now if you put your mind to it, some of which is ably assisted by friends.

5 MONDAY
Moon Age Day 27   Moon Sign Libra

This might not be the best day for personal gain but there are some areas of life that work better for you than others. For example, all romantic possibilities are highlighted right now, even though from a material point of view extra care is necessary. Friends can be guaranteed to come up trumps at this time.

6 TUESDAY
Moon Age Day 28   Moon Sign Libra

There are probably good things happening on the social horizon and you ought to be in a good position to gain from them today. Although your commitment to work is somewhat limited when compared with the recent past, you will do what is expected of you and can be guaranteed to offer timely advice to others.

7 WEDNESDAY
Moon Age Day 0   Moon Sign Scorpio

Much energy now goes into getting exactly what you want from life. A few people could accuse you of being somewhat ruthless right now, though that isn't really the truth of the situation. Rather you have your heart set on certain goals and won't take kindly to being diverted at all.

8 THURSDAY
Moon Age Day 1   Moon Sign Scorpio

A period of high energy is here. Don't try to get going too quickly though, or you will overcrowd your schedule and get nothing done as a result. Slow and steady wins the race, at least early in the day. Later on you can pull out all the stops when looking at something very close to your own heart.

9 FRIDAY
Moon Age Day 2   Moon Sign Sagittarius

An enjoyable time could be had if you indulge in outdoor pursuits of one sort or another. Clearly the more competitive elements in your nature are showing and you really do want to win at the moment. This trend isn't restricted to recreation however and will show itself clearly at work too.

10 SATURDAY   *Moon Age Day 3   Moon Sign Sagittarius*

Though you might be taking on more than is strictly good for you this Saturday, there is little doubt about your resilience or your ability to see things through to their logical conclusion. There is a tendency for you to go it alone in situations that don't really demand this sort of approach.

11 SUNDAY   *Moon Age Day 4   Moon Sign Sagittarius*

A socially motivated period continues, though of course that isn't at all strange for your zodiac sign, so you may not even notice much difference. Whispering words of love into the right ear could prove interesting today and will show your partner how you really feel during a busy period.

12 MONDAY   *Moon Age Day 5   Moon Sign Capricorn*

A sense of freedom is vitally important now and you won't take kindly to being thwarted when it matters the most to get your own way. Travel could be uppermost in your mind and it is clear that you have a particular vision regarding the future. A degree of compromise is called for, but not too much.

13 TUESDAY   *Moon Age Day 6   Moon Sign Capricorn*

Loved ones and intimates require careful handling today. Your knockabout sense of humour probably won't be all that appropriate and you could do with showing a degree of patience, especially with people whose thought processes are not as quick as your own. Create interesting interludes for family members.

14 WEDNESDAY   *Moon Age Day 7   Moon Sign Aquarius*

Your potential for good luck is well marked at this time and continues unabated for a couple of days. Although you won't always be able to do things in quite the way you would wish right now, it's only a matter of time before you get your own way. A combination of determination and persuasion are your best weapons.

15 THURSDAY   *Moon Age Day 8   Moon Sign Aquarius*

Don't leave major decisions until later. Get them out of the way just as soon as you can. You are moving forward on all fronts and can make this a highly enjoyable sort of Thursday. Stay clear of domestic disputes, most of which have nothing to do with you in the first place. Concentrate on having fun.

16 FRIDAY   *Moon Age Day 9   Moon Sign Aquarius*

The emphasis today is on life's more playful aspects. Taking anything particularly seriously is going to be hard, at least until after next Wednesday. However, your offbeat sense of humour and off-the-wall attitude will be popular with almost everyone and can actually see you achieving a great deal.

17 SATURDAY   ☿   *Moon Age Day 10   Moon Sign Pisces*

Be careful when it comes to listening to gossip. There is a good chance that much of what you hear today is either misleading or downright wrong. Instead, opt for some fresh air if you can. This is Saturday after all and locking yourself inside the house won't be good for you, mentally or physically.

18 SUNDAY   ☿   *Moon Age Day 11   Moon Sign Pisces*

There ought to be pleasure coming from anything that means getting out of a rut. You won't take kindly to being tied down at the moment and will function better if you have room to breathe and to move. Even casual conversations can have quite far-reaching and positive implications.

19 MONDAY   ☿   *Moon Age Day 12   Moon Sign Aries*

Find something new and interesting with which you can start the week. The more entertaining you find life to be, the better you are likely to deal with it. Also, stand by to enter a new period in terms of relationships during which the motives of others become easier to understand.

20 TUESDAY ☿ *Moon Age Day 13   Moon Sign Aries*

This is a day during which you will want to speed ahead. Obstacles placed in your path can be got around because it won't do you much good to face them head on at present. If one person doesn't like what you have to say, find someone else. Perseverance and determination can work wonders.

21 WEDNESDAY ☿ *Moon Age Day 14   Moon Sign Taurus*

Your confidence tends to be fairly high, even if action is somewhat subdued. You won't have long to wait for things to get moving again and in the meantime, you can enjoy watching life go by, rather than having to be at the front of every queue. Concern for family members could be great but is probably not justified.

22 THURSDAY ☿ *Moon Age Day 15   Moon Sign Taurus*

This is a day to broaden your mind. There are a few complications possible but each of them teaches you something more about life and the best way to live it. Boredom is probably not on the cards and it appears you are finding newer and better ways to show both your affection and genuine concern.

23 FRIDAY ☿ *Moon Age Day 16   Moon Sign Taurus*

The instinct for skilful money-making is strong at the moment. There are ways and means to bring more cash into your life and you will recognise most of them. Although you could be finding the going a little tough in terms of casual friendships, the people who love you the most won't let you down.

24 SATURDAY ☿ *Moon Age Day 17   Moon Sign Gemini*

Your charming and playful side is now clearly on display. Don't be too distracted by the fun and games that are available because there is plenty for you to do in practical sense. Trends also suggest that many Aquarians may now be looking at the possibility of making changes to their living environments.

25 SUNDAY ☿ *Moon Age Day 18 Moon Sign Gemini*

The sort of input you receive today could prove very significant and since you are now paying more attention to the world at large, your ears and eyes are wide open. This might be a Sunday but you can still make general progress. The days ahead look interesting and potentially lucrative.

26 MONDAY ☿ *Moon Age Day 19 Moon Sign Cancer*

It looks as though professional matters are well starred at the moment, even if it doesn't seem to be that way at first. When you are faced with awkward people today, turn on that natural charm and watch situations change quickly. You might have to show a good deal of give and take in romantic attachments.

27 TUESDAY ☿ *Moon Age Day 20 Moon Sign Cancer*

There should be a greater sense of adventure showing itself today, which is something of a pity, bearing in mind that the month's lunar low begins tomorrow. For the moment, push forward progressively and embrace change. Relationships ought to be working especially well at the moment.

28 WEDNESDAY ☿ *Moon Age Day 21 Moon Sign Leo*

There is a temporary lull beginning today. You don't want it and will fight against it but facts are facts. What you can do very well at the moment is to think. Looking ahead, making plans and getting yourself into a more favourable position generally is going to be both important and relevant.

29 THURSDAY ☿ *Moon Age Day 22 Moon Sign Leo*

The fewer mistakes you make today, the better you are going to feel about life as a whole. Concentration won't be all that easy but you will win through if you employ a degree of dogged determination. Don't necessarily expect a high degree of co-operation, even from people who usually lend a hand.

30 FRIDAY ☿ *Moon Age Day 23   Moon Sign Virgo*

Work and professional matters should prove more than fulfilling.
Even if you don't have to toil professionally today you will find
something to keep you occupied. Physical activity is very good for
you, as long as you don't do the usual Air sign trick and overdo it.
Moderation in all things is the key.

December
2018

1 SATURDAY ☿ *Moon Age Day 24   Moon Sign Virgo*

This is the first day of December and you won't want to let any opportunity pass you by at this time. From a social point of view the day can be very enjoyable and you know what you want from new encounters. Don't be slow to ask for a favour, particularly from people who are always willing to lend a hand.

2 SUNDAY ☿ *Moon Age Day 25   Moon Sign Libra*

Your go-getting side is certainly showing at present. With masses of energy, an original way of seeing things and plenty of charm, you should have little difficulty impressing some pretty important people. Although a good time socially speaking, today could also involve work or practical issues at home.

3 MONDAY ☿ *Moon Age Day 26   Moon Sign Libra*

Personal indulgences would be good today but there isn't really all that much time to enjoy them. You are able to succeed, on occasion against some very formidable odds. In a way the more difficult situations are, the better you like them right now. Avoid dull routines, which hold little for you at present.

4 TUESDAY ☿ *Moon Age Day 27   Moon Sign Scorpio*

Though your love life might not be offering everything you would wish, it is possible to pep things up with just a little effort on your part. Any minor health problems should be less emphasised now, particularly since you are willing to take things easily, even passing on some responsibilities.

5 WEDNESDAY ☿ *Moon Age Day 28   Moon Sign Scorpio*

When it comes to matters associated with money it appears that your rather happy-go-lucky nature isn't so useful at present. You need to count the pennies carefully, making certain that you are not taking financial risks or spending needlessly on luxuries you don't even really want.

6 THURSDAY ☿ *Moon Age Day 29   Moon Sign Scorpio*

An important plan could miss the target unless you make absolutely sure of all the details. It can't be stressed enough now how important it is to check and double-check everything. If you are careful, something you have wanted for ages could be coming your way at any time now.

7 FRIDAY *Moon Age Day 0   Moon Sign Sagittarius*

This is certainly not a time during which you should be taking anything for granted. You need to be sure of your facts, especially before you shoot your mouth off in any public forum. Today does offer significant diversions, plus the chance to really impress someone you rate highly.

8 SATURDAY *Moon Age Day 1   Moon Sign Sagittarius*

In the build-up to all the fun and games you are likely to be the life and soul of any party you go to. You should be doing your fair share of entertaining too, and will be quite happy to mix with a broad cross-section of society. Don't be surprised if you find yourself in the limelight at some stage today.

9 SUNDAY *Moon Age Day 2   Moon Sign Capricorn*

Your social life generally, and your association with people you love especially, sets today apart as being quite special. There is a quiet side to your nature all the same and you might choose to spend some time watching a classic old movie, or maybe reading a good book. Don't be surprised if you are very nostalgic today.

10 MONDAY
Moon Age Day 3   Moon Sign Capricorn

Relationships can be something of a struggle to deal with at the beginning of this working week. In games of chance, or sporting activities, you clearly have your wits about you and can make great gains. Don't gloat over your successes, though. It isn't necessary and only cheapens your winning streak.

11 TUESDAY
Moon Age Day 4   Moon Sign Aquarius

The lunar high is really on your side this time around, making this perhaps the best interlude during the whole of December. Give and take in family matters is noticed and helps you make some important allies. Affairs of the heart are positively highlighted and it isn't at all hard to make a good impression.

12 WEDNESDAY
Moon Age Day 5   Moon Sign Aquarius

When it comes to voicing your opinions it appears that you are only too willing to have your say. Good fortune is still on your side, but you may tend to push your luck somewhat more than is good for you. Try to curb your enthusiasm just a little and don't be too quick to volunteer for anything.

13 THURSDAY
Moon Age Day 6   Moon Sign Aquarius

Though your dealings with people in the wider world ought to be going well, there is a chance that you won't be making too good an impression on family members. Perhaps they find you pushy or unwilling to see their point of view. Whatever the truth of the situation you need to look at your responses carefully.

14 FRIDAY
Moon Age Day 7   Moon Sign Pisces

Stand by for a busy day, but one that can be quite rewarding, especially from a financial point of view. You are not afraid to put in the hard work necessary in order to get ahead, even though not everyone around you is equally helpful. Confidence counts, especially in the eyes of others.

15 SATURDAY
Moon Age Day 8   Moon Sign Pisces

Although you can't have everything you would wish today, you can come very close to it. The fact is that your powers of communication are very good and so asking for what you want isn't at all difficult. Who can resist that Aquarian charm? Not the people who count most, that's for certain.

16 SUNDAY
Moon Age Day 9   Moon Sign Pisces

Encounters with people who come new into your life could prove to be something of an inspiration now. Someone somewhere seeks to offer you some timely advice and it would be at least sensible to listen, even if you decide to follow your own path in any case. All in all, this should be a positive day.

17 MONDAY
Moon Age Day 10   Moon Sign Aries

Simple conversation is what proves to be most useful today. The things you hear as you go about from place to place could inspire you in some way and might lead to ideas that can mature in the fullness of time. Although you can be of tremendous use to friends there are some things you cannot do for them.

18 TUESDAY
Moon Age Day 11   Moon Sign Aries

The present position of the Sun is still supporting you in your struggle to make necessary changes, not least of all those associated with your working life. Your day is likely to be polarised because the working Aquarius everyone sees right now is so radically different from the person you are when enjoying yourself.

19 WEDNESDAY
Moon Age Day 12   Moon Sign Taurus

When it comes to organising your home life, you are extremely co-operative and anxious to show just how giving you can be. This is in stark contrast to the more practical qualities you possess. However, there could be a few people around who find this polarity of nature difficult to understand.

20 THURSDAY   *Moon Age Day 13   Moon Sign Taurus*

Gradually, you find yourself identifying more with the needs and aspirations of the group and that means as the month wears on any recent solitary tendencies are inclined to disappear. The quirky side of Aquarius begins to show more, though in ways that make your relatives and friends smile.

21 FRIDAY   *Moon Age Day 14   Moon Sign Gemini*

Your general manner can be blunter than might be expected for Aquarius so you need to exercise a good deal of patience when dealing with people who are naturally inclined to get on your nerves. You can easily use present trends to get ahead, though you probably need to lighten up somewhat.

22 SATURDAY   *Moon Age Day 15   Moon Sign Gemini*

This ought to be a good period for getting about socially and for finding new ways to enjoy yourself. Perhaps you are already in the middle of festive social occasions, or else pepping up the romantic side of your life. Whatever your choice, life finds ways and means to accommodate you.

23 SUNDAY   *Moon Age Day 16   Moon Sign Cancer*

This is a day on which it would be wise to follow your instincts, which are unlikely to let you down. Although not everyone you meet at present is equally reliable, it ought to be fairly easy for you to sort out the wheat from the chaff. Turn up your intuition and listen carefully to what it is telling you.

24 MONDAY   *Moon Age Day 17   Moon Sign Cancer*

Christmas Eve may not be a slow going day; in fact before it is over you could have tired yourself out. Spread your efforts socially and don't let people monopolise you. The fact is that family and friends deserve at least some of your time, particularly younger people at this special time of year.

25 TUESDAY   *Moon Age Day 18   Moon Sign Leo*

A rest period is called for, and Christmas Day offers all the right circumstances to get one. Don't rush around recklessly, but be willing to allow others to take some of the strain. You should find that you have friends who care about you deeply, as well as relatives who are quite willing to put themselves out on your account.

26 WEDNESDAY   *Moon Age Day 19   Moon Sign Leo*

Although the lull patch is still in operation, things ought to speed up noticeably towards the middle of the day. That old friend of yours, wanderlust, begins to play a part in your thinking and you won't take kindly to be being trapped in situations you see as being distinctly boring.

27 THURSDAY   *Moon Age Day 20   Moon Sign Virgo*

What really sets today apart is the way your typical Aquarian nature can so easily bring out the best in others. You have plenty to keep you busy, both inside the family and further afield. This is unlikely to be a totally stay-at-home sort of day for many Aquarians and excitement is quite possible.

28 FRIDAY   *Moon Age Day 21   Moon Sign Virgo*

Getting along well in group situations isn't as easy now as it might have seemed to be only a few days ago. You have to adjust to a twelfth house Sun, whilst at the same time not giving people around you the impression you are being aloof. Stand by for a few complaints from family members if you refuse to join in with the fun.

29 SATURDAY   *Moon Age Day 22   Moon Sign Libra*

For some of you there is likely to be a new or renewed romantic interest to think about. The vast majority of Aquarians will be fully committed to having a good time, particularly this evening. A few family responsibilities may crowd in during the day but you will find time later to pop a few corks.

30 SUNDAY   *Moon Age Day 23   Moon Sign Libra*

You can afford to exploit the general good luck that surrounds you at present and it is more or less certain that your organisational skills are well honed for the moment. It appears you are now better at expressing your opinions in ways that others find easier to understand and you are clearly exhibiting your sense of fun.

31 MONDAY   *Moon Age Day 24   Moon Sign Libra*

The last day of the year finds you more enthusiastic than ever and quite happy to take on any amount of new responsibilities. You see the year ahead as being a good road that can lead to exciting destinations. So positive is your attitude at present, almost everyone you meet will want to be your friend.

RISING SIGNS FOR AQUARIUS

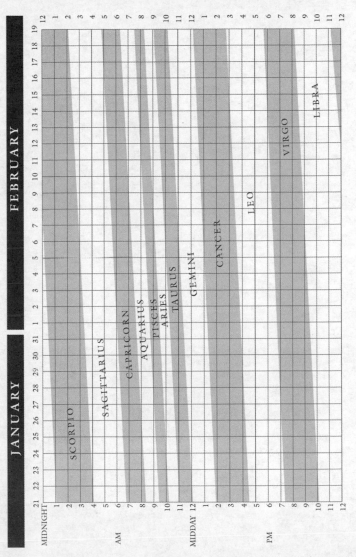

157

THE ZODIAC, PLANETS AND CORRESPONDENCES

The Earth revolves around the Sun once every calendar year, so when viewed from Earth the Sun appears in a different part of the sky as the year progresses. In astrology, these parts of the sky are divided into the signs of the zodiac and this means that the signs are organised in a circle. The circle begins with Aries and ends with Pisces.

Taking the zodiac sign as a starting point, astrologers then work with all the positions of planets, stars and many other factors to calculate horoscopes and birth charts and tell us what the stars have in store for us.

The table below shows the planets and Elements for each of the signs of the zodiac. Each sign belongs to one of the four Elements: Fire, Air, Earth or Water. Fire signs are creative and enthusiastic; Air signs are mentally active and thoughtful; Earth signs are constructive and practical; Water signs are emotional and have strong feelings.

It also shows the metals and gemstones associated with, or corresponding with, each sign. The correspondence is made when a metal or stone possesses properties that are held in common with a particular sign of the zodiac.

Finally, the table shows the opposite of each star sign – this is the opposite sign in the astrological circle.

Placed	Sign	Symbol	Element	Planet	Metal	Stone	Opposite
1	Aries	Ram	Fire	Mars	Iron	Bloodstone	Libra
2	Taurus	Bull	Earth	Venus	Copper	Sapphire	Scorpio
3	Gemini	Twins	Air	Mercury	Mercury	Tiger's Eye	Sagittarius
4	Cancer	Crab	Water	Moon	Silver	Pearl	Capricorn
5	Leo	Lion	Fire	Sun	Gold	Ruby	Aquarius
6	Virgo	Maiden	Earth	Mercury	Mercury	Sardonyx	Pisces
7	Libra	Scales	Air	Venus	Copper	Sapphire	Aries
8	Scorpio	Scorpion	Water	Pluto	Plutonium	Jasper	Taurus
9	Sagittarius	Archer	Fire	Jupiter	Tin	Topaz	Gemini
10	Capricorn	Goat	Earth	Saturn	Lead	Black Onyx	Cancer
11	Aquarius	Waterbearer	Air	Uranus	Uranium	Amethyst	Leo
12	Pisces	Fishes	Water	Neptune	Tin	Moonstone	Virgo